quick-method QUILTS

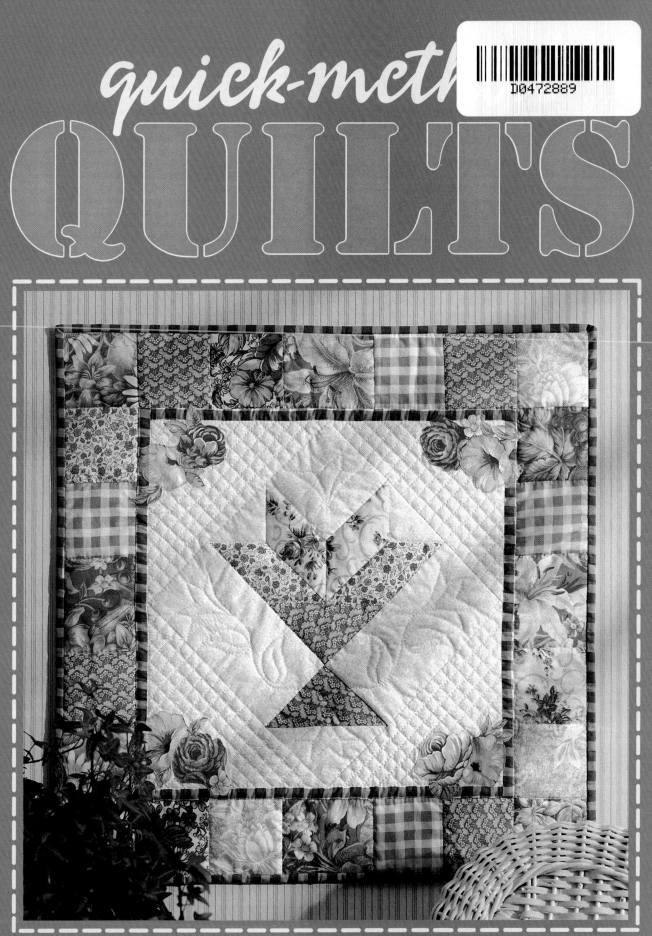

LEISURE ARTS, INC.
LITTLE ROCK, ARKANSAS

INTRODUCTION

Now you have time to make beautiful quilts in the traditional patterns of yesteryear — thanks to the time-saving methods you'll learn in Quick-Method Quilts! In our new book, we don't just speed up bygone ways; we use nifty shortcuts and contemporary methods to re-create a host of classic patterns! We also include helpful tips that simplify your quilting, and we even rate the skill levels of our quilts, so you can select a project that's right for you. If your schedule still doesn't allow time for making a full-size quilt, you can enjoy our smaller coordinating projects, such as wall hangings, pillows, window treatments, and decorated clothing. These give you the fun of making quilted items, but in a fraction of the time. With this handy guide at your fingertips, it's now easier than ever before to create the beautiful patchwork you've always admired!

TABLE OF CONTENTS

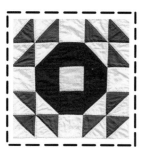

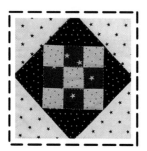

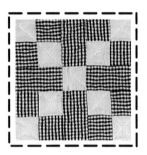

CHURN DASH COLLECTION

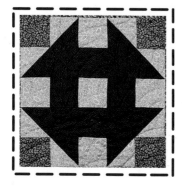

The classic Churn Dash, as with many traditional quilts, was inspired by an aspect of daily life in the olden days. Its resemblance to old-fashioned butter churns gave us this name, but we also know the pattern by such colorful titles as Monkey Wrench, Hole in the Barn Door, and Lincoln's Platform. To re-create the antique Churn Dash variation quilt shown here, we simplified the fabric choices and used a combination of easy strip piecing and unit piecing to make the bold blocks. Simple sashing strips, offset with nine-patch sashing blocks, and Baptist fan quilting provide more charming detail.

Our reversible wall hanging provides two decorative accents in one! The warm color scheme is carried out in four easily strip-pieced blocks and sashing strips on the front. Simply turn the wall hanging over to reveal an oversized Churn Dash block on the back. Decorative quilting using the Baptist fan pattern — also known as shells — completes the traditional look.

CHURN DASH VARIATION QUILT

SKILL LEVEL: 1 2 3 4 5
BLOCK SIZE: 13³/₄" x 13³/₄"
QUILT SIZE: 63" x 83"

Our antique quilt features several different scrap fabrics in each color family. Our quick-method instructions simplify the color choices by using a single print for each color family.

YARDAGE REQUIREMENTS

Yardage is based on 45"w fabric.

- ¹/₂ yd of maroon print
- ⁷/₈ yd of red print
- 1¹/₈ yds of cream print
- 1¹/₄ yds of blue print
- 4 yds of tan print
  5¹/₄ yds for backing
  1 yd for binding
  72" x 90" batting

CUTTING OUT THE PIECES

All measurements include a ¹/₄" seam allowance. Follow Rotary Cutting, page 144, to cut fabric.

1. **From maroon print:** ■
   - Cut 4 selvage-to-selvage strips 3¹/₄"w. From these strips, cut a total of 48 **squares** 3¹/₄" x 3¹/₄".

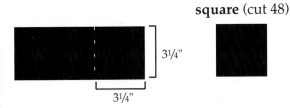

square (cut 48)

2. **From red print:** ■
   - Cut 11 selvage-to-selvage **strips** 2¹/₂"w.

3. **From cream print:** ▢
   - Cut 5 selvage-to-selvage **strips** 3¹/₄"w.
   - Cut 5 selvage-to-selvage strips 3⁵/₈"w. From these strips, cut a total of 48 squares 3⁵/₈" x 3⁵/₈". Cut squares once diagonally to make 96 **triangles**.

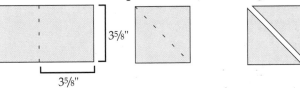

square (cut 48)   **triangle** (cut 96)

4. **From blue print:** ■
   - Cut 4 selvage-to-selvage **strips** 3¹/₄"w.
   - Cut 4 selvage-to-selvage strips 6³/₈"w. From these strips, cut a total of 24 squares 6³/₈" x 6³/₈". Cut squares once diagonally to make 48 **triangles**.

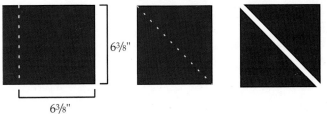

square (cut 24)   **triangle** (cut 48)

5. **From tan print:** ▨
   - Cut 19 selvage-to-selvage **strips** 2¹/₂"w.
   - Cut 2 lengthwise strips 5" x 85" for **side borders**.
   - Cut 2 lengthwise strips 5" x 55" for **top/bottom borders**.

ASSEMBLING THE QUILT TOP

Follow Piecing and Pressing, page 146, to make quilt top.

1. Assemble 1 **square** and 2 **triangles** as shown to make **Unit 1**. Make 48 **Unit 1's**.

Unit 1 (make 48)

2. Assemble 1 **Unit 1** and 1 **triangle** as shown to make **Unit 2**. Make 48 **Unit 2's**.

Unit 2 (make 48)

3. Assemble **strips** as shown to make **Strip Set A**. Make 2 **Strip Set A's**. Cut across **Strip Set A's** at 3¼" intervals to make a total of 24 **Unit 3's**.

Strip Set A (make 2)   **Unit 3** (make 24)

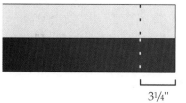

3¼"

4. Assemble 2 **Unit 2's** and 1 **Unit 3** as shown to make **Unit 4**. Make 24 **Unit 4's**.

Unit 4 (make 24)

5. Assemble **strips** as shown to make 1 **Strip Set B**. Cut across **Strip Set B** at 3¼" intervals to make a total of 12 **Unit 5's**.

Strip Set B (make 1)   **Unit 5** (make 12)

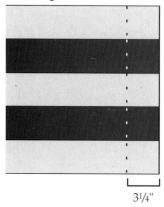

3¼"

6. Assemble 2 **Unit 4's** and 1 **Unit 5** as shown to make **Block**. Make 12 **Blocks**.

Block (make 12)

7. Assemble **strips** as shown to make **Strip Set C**. Make 9 **Strip Set C's**.

Strip Set C (make 9)

8. Cut across **Strip Set C's** at 14¼" intervals to make a total of 17 **Sashing Strip Sets**. Cut across remaining **Strip Set C** lengths at 2½" intervals to make a total of 6 **Unit 6's**.

Sashing Strip Set (make 17)   **Unit 6** (make 6)

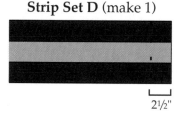

14¼"   2½"

9. Assemble **strips** as shown to make 1 **Strip Set D**. Cut across **Strip Set D** at 2½" intervals to make a total of 12 **Unit 7's**.

Strip Set D (make 1)   **Unit 7** (make 12)

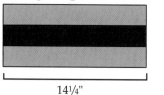

2½"

10. Assemble 2 **Unit 7's** and 1 **Unit 6** as shown to make **Sashing Block**. Make 6 **Sashing Blocks**.

Sashing Block (make 6)

11. Assemble 3 **Blocks** and 2 **Sashing Strip Sets** as shown to make **Row**. Make 4 **Rows**.

Row (make 4)

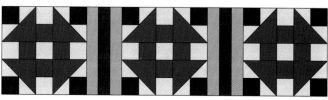

12. Assemble 3 **Sashing Strip Sets** and 2 **Sashing Blocks** as shown to make **Sashing Row**. Make 3 **Sashing Rows**.

Sashing Row (make 3)

13. Referring to **Quilt Top Diagram**, assemble **Rows** and **Sashing Rows** to complete center section of quilt top.
14. Follow **Adding Squared Borders**, page 150, and **Quilt Top Diagram** to add **top**, **bottom**, and then **side borders** to complete **Quilt Top**. Round off corners as shown.

COMPLETING THE QUILT

1. Follow **Quilting**, page 151, and **Quilting Diagram** to mark, layer, and quilt. To mark each "Baptist fan" quilting pattern, use a compass to mark 5 arcs $3/4$" apart on border of quilt and 6 arcs $3/4$" apart on center section of quilt.
2. Cut a 36" square of binding fabric. Follow **Making Continuous Bias Strip Binding**, page 155, to make approximately $8^{1}/_{2}$ yds of $2^{1}/_{2}$"w bias binding.
3. Follow Steps 1 and 2 of **Attaching Binding with Mitered Borders**, page 155, to pin binding to quilt. Using a $1/4$" seam allowance, sew binding to quilt. Fold binding over to quilt backing; blindstitch in place.

Quilting Diagram

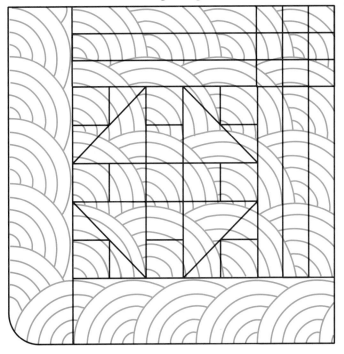

Quilt Top Diagram

- - - **QUICK TIP** - - -

USING PRECUT QUILTING STENCILS

Use a precut quilting stencil to make marking your quilt faster and easier. Plastic precut stencils are available at your favorite quilting store and come in a variety of classic designs. You'll probably find ones that closely match many of the quilting designs in this book, such as the "Baptist fan" pattern featured on the Churn Dash Variation Quilt here and the cable and feather patterns used on our LeMoyne Star Quilt shown on page 117. As an added bonus, the stencils are usually inexpensive and reusable!

13

CHURN DASH WALL HANGING

SKILL LEVEL: 1 2 3 4 5
BLOCK SIZE: 11¼" x 11¼"
WALL HANGING SIZE: 37" x 37"

YARDAGE REQUIREMENTS

Yardage is based on 45"w fabric.

- ⬛ ³/₈ yd of maroon print
- 🔲 ³/₄ yd of tan print
- ⬛ 1 yd of blue print
- ⬛ 1 yd of dark maroon print
- ⬛ 1¼ yds of brown print
  ⁷/₈ yd for binding and hanging loops
  41"x 41" batting

CUTTING OUT THE PIECES

All measurements include a ¹/₄" seam allowance. Follow
Rotary Cutting, *page 144, to cut fabric.*

1. **From maroon print:**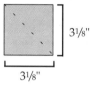
    - Cut 2 selvage-to-selvage strips 2³/₄"w. From these strips, cut a total of 16 **small squares** 2³/₄" x 2³/₄".

    small square (cut 16)

    2³/₄"
    2³/₄"

    - Cut 1 selvage-to-selvage strip 5¹/₂"w. From this strip, cut a total of 4 **large squares** 5¹/₂" x 5¹/₂".

    large square (cut 4)

    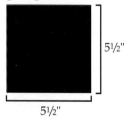
    5¹/₂"
    5¹/₂"

2. **From tan print:**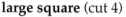
    - Cut 2 selvage-to-selvage **strips** 2³/₄"w.
    - Cut 4 **small squares** 2³/₄" x 2³/₄".

    small square (cut 4)

    2³/₄"
    2³/₄"

- Cut 2 selvage-to-selvage strips 3¹/₈"w. From these strips, cut a total of 16 squares 3¹/₈" x 3¹/₈". Cut squares once diagonally to make 32 **small triangles**.

square (cut 16)   **small triangle** (cut 32)

3¹/₈"
3¹/₈"

- Cut 1 selvage-to-selvage strip 5¹/₂"w. From this strip, cut 1 **large square** 5¹/₂" x 5¹/₂". Remainder of strip will be used to make Strip Set D.

large square (cut 1)

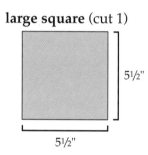
5¹/₂"
5¹/₂"

- Cut 1 selvage-to-selvage strip 5⁷/₈"w. From this strip, cut a total of 4 squares 5⁷/₈" x 5⁷/₈". Cut squares once diagonally to make 8 **large triangles**.

square (cut 4)   **large triangle** (cut 8)

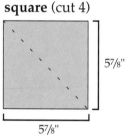   
5⁷/₈"
5⁷/₈"

3. **From blue print:**
    - Cut 2 selvage-to-selvage **strips** 2³/₄"w.
    - Cut 2 selvage-to-selvage strips 5³/₈"w. From these strips, cut a total of 8 squares 5³/₈" x 5³/₈". Cut squares once diagonally to make 16 **small triangles**.

    square (cut 8)   **small triangle** (cut 16)

    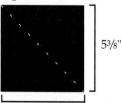
    5³/₈"
    5³/₈"

14

- Cut 1 selvage-to-selvage **strip** 5½"w.
- Cut 1 selvage-to-selvage strip 10⅞"w. From this strip, cut a total of 2 squares 10⅞" x 10⅞". Cut squares once diagonally to make 4 **large triangles**.

square (cut 2)

10⅞"

10⅞"

large triangle (cut 4)

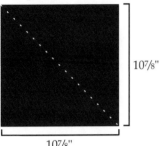

4. **From dark maroon print:**
   - Cut 11 selvage-to-selvage **strips** 2"w.
   - Cut 1 selvage-to-selvage strip 6"w. From this strip, cut a total of 4 **squares** 6" x 6".

square (cut 4)

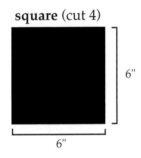

6"

6"

5. **From brown print:**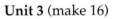
   - Cut 11 selvage-to-selvage **strips** 2"w.
   - Cut 8 selvage-to-selvage **strips** 2½"w.

ASSEMBLING THE WALL HANGING

*Follow **Piecing and Pressing**, page 146, to make wall hanging front and back.*

WALL HANGING FRONT

1. Assemble 2 **small triangles** and 1 **small square** as shown to make **Unit 1**. Make 16 **Unit 1's**.

Unit 1 (make 16)

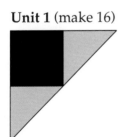

2. Assemble 1 **small triangle** and 1 **Unit 1** as shown to make **Unit 2**. Make 16 **Unit 2's**.

Unit 2 (make 16)

3. Assemble **strips** as shown to make **Strip Set A**. Make 2 **Strip Set A's**. Cut across **Strip Set A's** at 2¾" intervals to make a total of 16 **Unit 3's**.

Strip Set A (make 2)

Unit 3 (make 16)

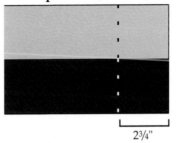

2¾"

4. Assemble 2 **Unit 2's** and 1 **Unit 3** as shown to make **Unit 4**. Make 8 **Unit 4's**.

Unit 4 (make 8)

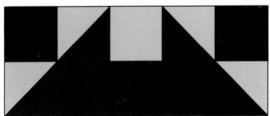

5. Assemble 2 **Unit 3's** and 1 **small square** as shown to make **Unit 5**. Make 4 **Unit 5's**.

Unit 5 (make 4)

6. Assemble 2 **Unit 4's** and 1 **Unit 5** as shown to make **Block A**. Make 4 **Block A's**.

Block A (make 4)

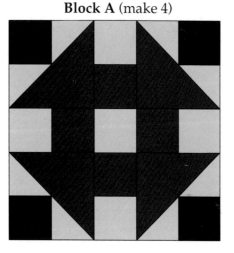

7. Assemble **strips** as shown to make 1 **Strip Set B**. Cut across **Strip Set B** at 2" intervals to make a total of 18 **Unit 6's**.

Strip Set B (make 1) **Unit 6** (make 18)

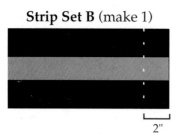
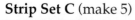

2"

8. Assemble **strips** as shown to make **Strip Set C**. Make 5 **Strip Set C's**. Cut across 1 **Strip Set C** at 2" intervals to make a total of 9 **Unit 7's**.

Strip Set C (make 5) **Unit 7** (make 9)

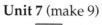

2"

9. Assemble 2 **Unit 6's** and 1 **Unit 7** as shown to make **Unit 8**. Make 9 **Unit 8's**.

Unit 8 (make 9)

10. Cut across remaining **Strip Set C's** at 11¾" intervals to make a total of 12 **Sashing Strip Sets**.

Sashing Strip Set (make 12)

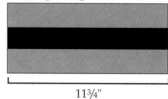

11¾"

11. Assemble 2 **Block A's** and 3 **Sashing Strip Sets** as shown to make **Row**. Make 2 **Rows**.

Row (make 2)

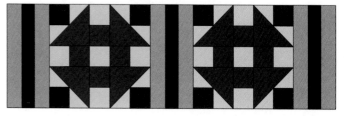

12. Assemble 3 **Unit 8's** and 2 **Sashing Strip Sets** as shown to make **Unit 9**. Make 3 **Unit 9's**.

Unit 9 (make 3)

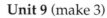

13. Assemble **Unit 9's** and **Rows** as shown to complete **Wall Hanging Front**.

Wall Hanging Front

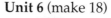

WALL HANGING BACK

1. Use 2 tan **large triangles**, 1 **square**, and 1 blue **large triangle** and repeat Steps 1 and 2 of **Wall Hanging Front**, page 15, to make **Unit 10** as shown. Make 4 **Unit 10's**.

Unit 10 (make 4)

2. Assemble **strips** as shown (strips are not the same length) to make **Strip Set D.** Cut across **Strip Set D** at 5¹/₂" intervals to make a total of 4 **Unit 11's**.

Strip Set D (make 1)   **Unit 11** (make 4)

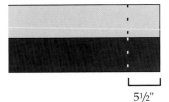 

5¹/₂"

3. Using **Unit 10's**, **Unit 11's**, and 1 **square**, repeat Steps 4 - 6 of **Wall Hanging Front**, page 15, to complete **Block B**.

Block B (make 1)

4. Assemble strips as shown to make **Strip Set E**. Make 4 **Strip Set E's**. Cut 1 piece 25¹/₂"l from each **Strip Set E** to make a total of 4 **Unit 12's**.

Strip Set E (make 4)   **Unit 12** (make 4)

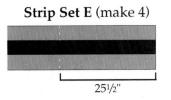 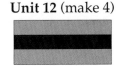

25¹/₂"

5. Assemble 1 **Unit 12** and 2 **squares** as shown to make **Border Strip Set**. Make 2 **Border Strip Sets**.

Border Strip Set (make 2)

6. Assemble **Unit 12's**, **Block B**, and **Border Strip Sets** as shown to complete **Wall Hanging Back**.

Wall Hanging Back

COMPLETING THE WALL HANGING

1. Follow **Quilting**, page 151, and **Quilting Diagram** to mark, layer, and quilt. To mark each "Baptist fan" quilting pattern, use a compass to mark 5 arcs ³/₄" apart.
2. For hanging loops, cut 1 selvage-to-selvage strip 5"w. Cut across strip at 6" intervals to make a total of 5 pieces 5" x 6". Match right sides and fold each piece in half lengthwise; sew long raw edges together. Turn right side out and press. Matching raw edges, fold each piece in half to form a loop. Referring to photo and spacing loops evenly, baste raw edges of loops to top raw edge of wall hanging back.
3. Cut a 27" square of binding fabric. Follow **Making Continuous Bias Strip Binding**, page 155, to make approximately 4¹/₄ yds of 2¹/₂"w bias binding.
4. Follow **Attaching Binding with Mitered Corners**, page 155, to attach binding to wall hanging.

Quilting Diagram

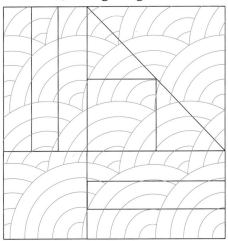

CROWN OF THORNS

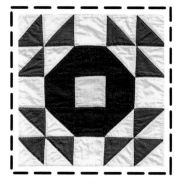

In the early years of America, women often gathered at the local church house for quilting bees, so it was only natural that patterns with Biblical themes became popular. The Crown of Thorns quilt shown here displays its traditional Amish design against a white background, symbolizing Christ's purity. To make this simple quilt even easier, our instructions call for rotary cutting and strip piecing, and a grid method makes the triangle-squares a breeze to put together. Alternating the patterned blocks with large white blocks saves time on piecing — and provides a dramatic showcase for the lovely feathered circle and lattice quilting.

CROWN OF THORNS QUILT

SKILL LEVEL: 1 2 3 4 5
BLOCK SIZE: 10" x 10"
QUILT SIZE: 76" x 76"

YARDAGE REQUIREMENTS

Yardage is based on 45"w fabric.

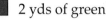 5½ yds of white
2 yds of green
1¼ yds of red
¼ yd of yellow
4¾ yds for backing
1 yd of green for binding
81" x 96" batting

CUTTING OUT THE PIECES

All measurements include a ¼" seam allowance. Follow Rotary Cutting, page 144, to cut fabric.

1. **From white:**
   - Cut 7 selvage-to-selvage **strips** 2½"w.
   - Cut 7 selvage-to-selvage strips 10½"w. From these strips, cut a total of 25 **setting squares** 10½" x 10½".

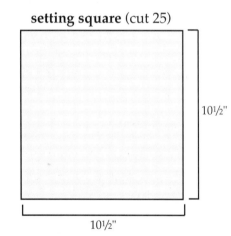

setting square (cut 25)

10½"

10½"

   - Cut 4 lengthwise strips 3" x 80" for **border**.
   - Cut 4 **squares** 22" x 22" from fabric width left after cutting borders.
2. **From green:**
   - Cut 3 **squares** 22" x 22".
3. **From red:**
   - Cut 7 selvage-to-selvage **strips** 2½"w.
   - Cut 1 **square** 22" x 22".
4. **From yellow:**
   - Cut 2 selvage-to-selvage **strips** 2½"w.

ASSEMBLING THE QUILT TOP

Follow Piecing and Pressing, page 146, to assemble quilt top.

1. To make **triangle-squares**, place 1 white and 1 red **square** right sides together. Referring to **Fig. 1**, follow Steps 1 - 3 of **Making Triangle-Squares**, page 146, to mark a grid of 49 squares 2⅞" x 2⅞". Referring to **Fig. 2** and starting and ending stitching as necessary, follow Steps 4 - 6 of **Making Triangle-Squares**, page 146, to complete 98 **triangle-squares** (you will need 96 and have 2 left over).

Fig. 1

2⅞"

2⅞"

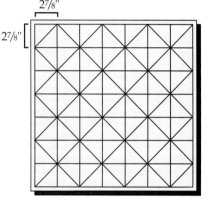

Fig. 2

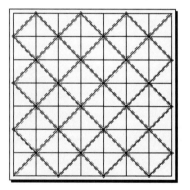

triangle-square (make 98)

2. Using white and green **squares**, repeat Step 1 to make a total of 294 **triangle-squares** (you will need 288 and have 6 left over).

triangle-square (make 294)

3. Assemble 4 **triangle-squares** as shown to make **Unit 1**. Make 96 **Unit 1's**.

Unit 1 (make 96)

4. Assemble 2¹⁄₂"w **strips** as shown to make **Strip Set A**. Make 3 **Strip Set A's**. Cut across **Strip Set A's** at 2¹⁄₂" intervals to make a total of 48 **Unit 2's**.

Strip Set A (make 3)   **Unit 2** (make 48)

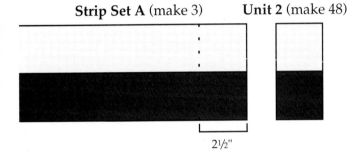

2¹⁄₂"

5. Assemble 2 **Unit 1's** and 1 **Unit 2** as shown to make **Unit 3**. Make 48 **Unit 3's**.

Unit 3 (make 48)

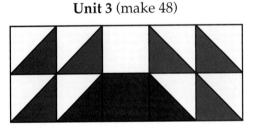

6. Assemble 2¹⁄₂"w **strips** as shown to make **Strip Set B**. Make 2 **Strip Set B's**. Cut across **Strip Set B's** at 2¹⁄₂" intervals to make a total of 24 **Unit 4's**.

Strip Set B (make 2)   **Unit 4** (make 24)

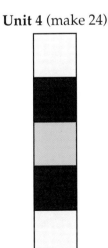

2¹⁄₂"

7. Assemble 2 **Unit 3's** and 1 **Unit 4** to make **Block**. Make 24 **Blocks**.

Block (make 24)

8. Assemble 4 **setting squares** and 3 **Blocks** as shown to make **Row A**. Make 4 **Row A's**.

Row A (make 4)

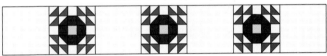

9. Assemble 4 **Blocks** and 3 **setting squares** as shown to make **Row B**. Make 3 **Row B's**.

Row B (make 3)

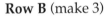
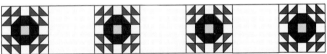

10. Referring to **Quilt Top Diagram**, page 22, assemble **Rows** to complete center section of quilt top.
11. Follow **Adding Mitered Borders**, page 150, and **Quilt Top Diagram**, page 22, to complete **Quilt Top**.

COMPLETING THE QUILT

1. Follow **Quilting**, page 151, **Quilting Diagram**, page 22, and **Quilting Patterns,** pages 22 and 23, to mark, layer, and quilt.
2. Cut a 36" square of binding fabric. Follow **Making Continuous Bias Strip Binding**, page 155, to make approximately 9 yds of 2¹⁄₂"w bias binding.
3. Follow **Attaching Binding with Mitered Corners**, page 155, to attach binding to quilt.

Quilt Top Diagram

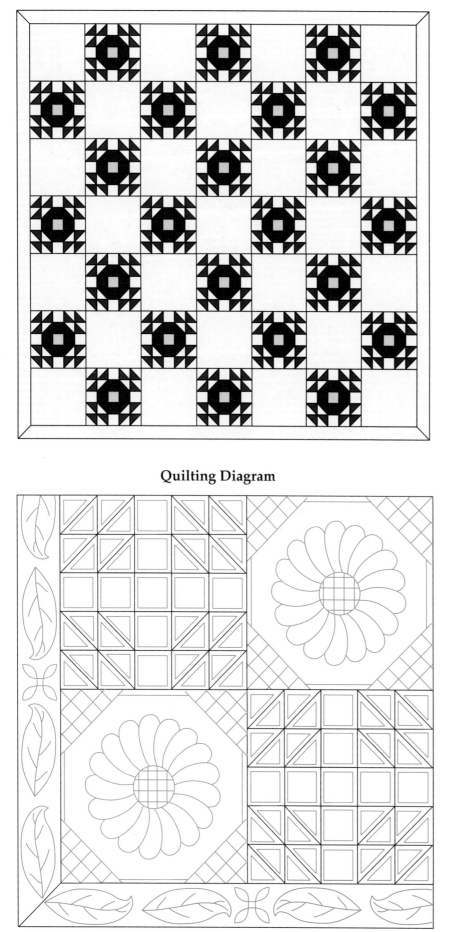

Quilting Pattern

Quilting Diagram

Quilting Pattern

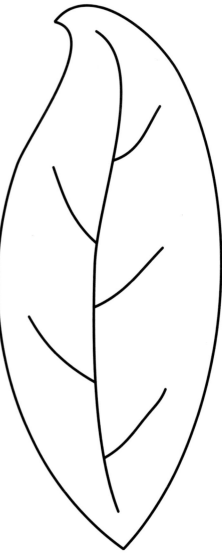

STRING COLLECTION

Following an era of prosperity when only "store-bought" goods were fashionable, the Great Depression forced a return to practical crafts such as quilting. Traditional patterns reemerged, but quilters also enjoyed an efficient new style called String quilting. Because families often couldn't spare the money for new fabrics, materials for these colorful mosaics were salvaged from every source — worn-out clothing, old bedding, and even flour sacks! The no-mistakes style of String quilting makes it a breeze for beginners to master. Just like this splendid antique, our version is made by randomly string piecing scrap fabrics to a muslin square, but we saved even more time by rotary cutting the "strings" to fit after sewing them on! Simple straight-line quilting provides a fitting finish to this carefree design.

Traditionally made from an array of many-colored scraps, String quilts take on a more elegant style when pieced with carefully selected fabrics in coordinating hues. The smaller scale of our lovely accessories lets you use a piecing method that's even easier than the way you make the quilt! Just sew strips of different fabrics together and then randomly cut out the shapes you need. A men's suit vest becomes feminine finery when its front panels are covered with string-pieced blocks and embellished with embroidery. (Opposite) The romance of our lace-trimmed wall hanging and sweet door pillow will tug at your heartstrings.

STRING QUILT

SKILL LEVEL: 1 2 3 4 5
BLOCK SIZE: 5" x 5"
QUILT SIZE: 71" x 81"

The nature of string quilting is such that different projects may vary greatly in appearance. Our instructions will produce a quilt similar to the antique quilt pictured, but with slightly more uniform pieces.

YARDAGE REQUIREMENTS
Yardage is based on 45"w fabric.

☐ 5³⁄₈ yds of muslin for foundation squares

◩ 7 yds **total** of assorted scrap fabrics
5 yds for backing
1 yd for binding
81" x 96" batting

CUTTING OUT THE PIECES
All measurements include a ¹⁄₄" seam allowance. Follow **Rotary Cutting**, *page 144, to cut fabric.*

1. **From muslin:**

   • Cut 32 selvage-to-selvage strips 5¹⁄₂"w. From these strips, cut a total of 224 **foundation squares** 5¹⁄₂" x 5¹⁄₂".

   foundation square (cut 224)

   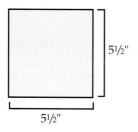

2. **From scrap fabrics:**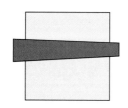

   • Cut scrap fabrics into **strips** ("strings") that vary from 1"w to 3"w and are at least 6" long. Strips should have straight edges but may be wider at 1 end than the other.

ASSEMBLING THE QUILT TOP
Follow **Piecing and Pressing**, *page 146, to make quilt top.*

1. Place 1 **strip** right side up across center of 1 **foundation square** (**Fig. 1**).

   Fig. 1

   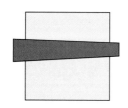

2. Place another **strip** wrong side up on first strip, matching strips along 1 long raw edge. Stitch both strips to foundation square along matched edge. Open second strip and press (**Fig. 2**).

   Fig. 2

3. Continue adding **strips**, stitching and pressing until foundation square is covered (**Fig. 3**).

   Fig. 3

   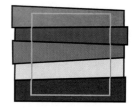

4. Place square on rotary cutting mat with strip-pieced side down. Referring to **Fig. 4**, use rotary cutter and ruler to trim ends of strips even with foundation square to complete **Block**.

   Fig. 4

   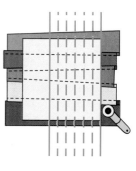

5. Repeat Steps 1 - 4 to make 224 **Blocks**.

   Block (make 224)

6. Alternating direction of strips in blocks vertically and horizontally, assemble 14 **Blocks** as shown to make **Row**. Make 16 **Rows**.

Row (make 16)

7. Referring to **Quilt Top Diagram**, sew **Rows** together to complete **Quilt Top**.

COMPLETING THE QUILT

1. Follow **Quilting**, page 151, and **Quilting Diagram** to mark, layer, and quilt.
2. Cut a 36" square of binding fabric. Follow **Making Continuous Bias Strip Binding**, page 155, to make approximately 9 yds of $2^1/2$"w bias binding.
3. Follow **Attaching Binding with Mitered Corners**, page 155, to attach binding to quilt.

Quilt Top Diagram

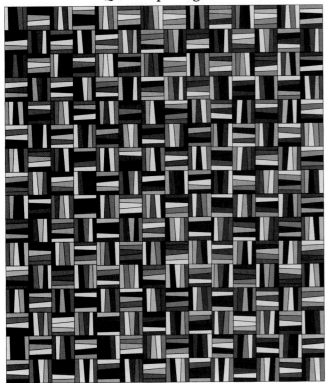

Quilting Diagram

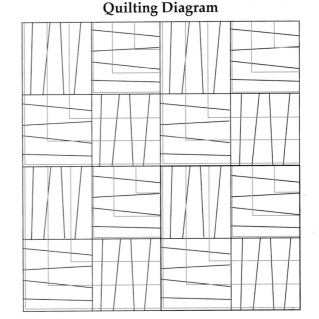

HEARTSTRINGS WALL HANGING

SKILL LEVEL: 1 2 3 4 5
SIZE: 14" x 23"

YARDAGE REQUIREMENTS

Yardage is based on 45" fabric.

▨ $3/4$ yd **total** of assorted cream prints

▨ $1/8$ yd of medium black plaid

▨ $1/4$ yd of small black plaid
$1/2$ yd for backing
$1/2$ yd for binding
18" x 27" batting

You will also need:

plastic template material
paper-backed fusible web
embroidery floss and/or silk ribbon
small pieces of lace, ribbon, buttons, and beads
  for embellishment

CUTTING OUT THE PIECES

All measurements include a $1/4$" seam allowance. Follow Rotary Cutting, page 146, to cut fabric.

1. **From assorted cream prints:** ▨
   • Cut selvage-to-selvage **strips** that vary from 1"w to 3"w.
2. **From medium black plaid:** ▨
   • Cut 2 **strips** 1" x $22^1/2$".
3. **From small black plaid:** ▨
   • Cut 1 **rectangle** $7^1/2$" x $22^1/2$".

ASSEMBLING THE WALL HANGING TOP

*Follow **Piecing and Pressing**, page 146, to make wall hanging top.*

1. Use a pencil to trace **Wall Hanging Heart Pattern**, page 33, onto paper side of fusible web 3 times. Cut out hearts on traced lines. From template material, cut one 3" x 5½" rectangle and one 3" x 2½" rectangle.
2. Sew cream **strips** together, arranging different widths and prints randomly, to form a rectangle approximately 18" x 45".
3. From one end of 18" x 45" rectangle, cut a 6" x 18" rectangle (**Fig. 1**). Follow manufacturer's instructions to fuse web hearts to wrong side of 6" x 18" rectangle at different angles (**Fig. 2**). Cut out hearts and remove paper backing.

Fig. 1

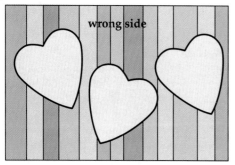

18"

6"

Fig. 2

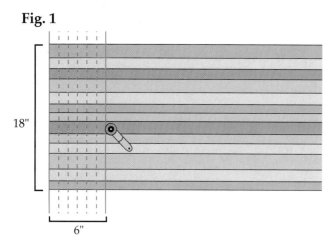

wrong side

4. Referring to photo and **Wall Hanging Top Diagram** and spacing hearts 2¼" apart, fuse hearts to center of plaid **rectangle**.
5. Use rectangle templates to trace eight 3" x 5½" rectangles and two 3" x 2½" rectangles at different angles onto remainder of strip-pieced fabric (**Fig. 3**). Cut out rectangles.

Fig. 3

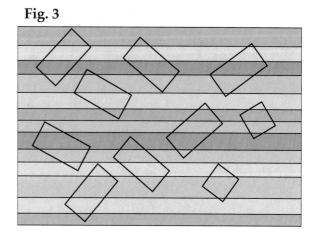

6. Assemble four 3" x 5½" rectangles and one 3" x 2½" rectangle as shown to make **Unit 1**. Make 2 **Unit 1's**.

Unit 1 (make 2)

7. Referring to **Wall Hanging Top Diagram**, assemble **Unit 1's**, plaid **strips**, and plaid **rectangle** to complete **Wall Hanging Top**.

COMPLETING THE WALL HANGING

1. Follow **Quilting**, page 151, to layer and quilt in the ditch around hearts and on each side of plaid strips.
2. Follow **Making a Hanging Sleeve**, page 157, to attach hanging sleeve to wall hanging.
3. Cut a 16" square of binding fabric. Follow **Making Continuous Bias Strip Binding**, page 155, to make approximately 2¼ yds of 2½"w bias binding.
4. Follow **Attaching Binding with Mitered Corners**, page 155, to attach binding to wall hanging.
5. Refer to **Embroidery Stitches**, page 158, and to photo to add embroidery to wall hanging. Embellish with lace, ribbon, buttons, and beads as desired.

Wall Hanging Top Diagram

STRING-PIECED VEST

SUPPLIES

Yardage is based on 45"w fabric.

 1½ yds **total** of assorted cream print fabrics

a men's suit vest (we found ours at a resale shop)

paper-backed fusible web

plastic template material

tracing paper

1 decorative button for each vest button

embroidery floss and/or silk ribbon for embroidery

small pieces of lace, ribbon, buttons, and beads for embellishment

MAKING THE VEST

1. Cut a square 5½" x 5½" from plastic template material.
2. Remove buttons from vest. Use seam ripper to take vest apart at shoulder and side seams. Set aside vest back.
3. To make pattern, place right vest front piece, right side up, on tracing paper. Use a pencil to draw around vest front piece; draw a second line ¼" outside the first. Cut out along outer line and label pattern. Repeat for left vest front piece.
4. Cut fabrics into selvage-to-selvage strips that vary from 1"w to 3"w. Follow Step 2 of **Assembling the Wall Hanging Top** for **Heartstrings Wall Hanging**, page 30, to make strip-pieced fabric.
5. Use square template and follow Step 5 of **Assembling the Wall Hanging Top** for **Heartstrings Wall Hanging**, page 30, to cut approximately 30 squares.
6. Using a ¼" seam allowance, assemble squares, alternating direction of strips, into a fabric piece large enough for right front vest pattern (**Fig. 1**). Repeat for left front vest pattern. Place each pattern, right side down, on wrong side of each fabric piece. Cut 1 piece using each pattern.

Fig. 1

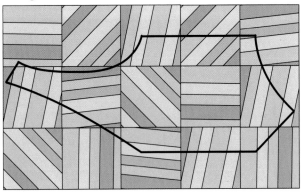

7. To make patterns for web, draw a third line ¼" inside first line on tracing paper patterns. Cut out along innermost lines. Place patterns, right side down, on paper backing side of web. Draw around each pattern and cut out along drawn lines. Center 1 web shape on wrong side of each fabric piece; fuse in place. Remove paper backing.
8. For each vest front piece, center fabric piece, right side up, on right side of vest front piece (fabric will extend past vest edges ¼"); fuse in place.
9. Press raw edges of fabric piece under ¼" so that pressed edges match edges of vest front piece. Topstitch in place through all layers.
10. Use a fabric marking pen to mark original placement of buttonholes and buttons along vest front pieces. Work buttonholes and cut open. Sew on decorative buttons.
11. To reassemble vest, refer to **Fig. 2** and insert shoulder and side seam allowances of vest front pieces between lining and outer fabric of vest back at shoulder and side seams. Topstitch through all layers.

Fig. 2

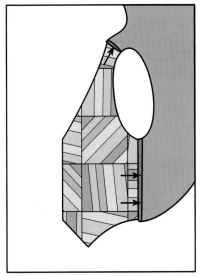

12. Refer to **Embroidery Stitches**, page 158, and to photo to add embroidery to vest front. Embellish with lace, ribbon, buttons, and beads as desired.

HAPPY HEART DOOR PILLOW

SIZE: 7" x 7"

SUPPLIES

8" x 8" fabric square of string-pieced, assorted cream prints (use leftover from projects in this section or refer to Step 2 of **Assembling the Wall Hanging Top** for **Heartstrings Wall Hanging**, page 30, to piece square)
$5^{1}/_{4}$" x $5^{1}/_{4}$" square of muslin
8" x 8" square of muslin for pillow top backing
8" x 8" square of fabric for pillow back
3" x 25" bias strip of plaid fabric for welting
5" x 5" square of paper-backed fusible web
8" x 8" square of batting
polyester fiberfill
25" of $^{1}/_{4}$" cord for welting
1 yd of $^{5}/_{8}$"w cream satin ribbon
two $^{5}/_{8}$" buttons
embroidery floss
beads
transparent monofilament thread
permanent fine-point marker
tracing paper

MAKING THE DOOR PILLOW

1. Fuse web to wrong side of $5^{1}/_{4}$" x $5^{1}/_{4}$" muslin square. Do not remove paper backing. Use permanent fine-point marker to trace **Happy Heart Pattern** onto muslin. Cut out just inside heart outline. Remove paper backing.
2. For pillow top pattern, trace **Large Heart Pattern** onto tracing paper; cut out. Position pattern on strip-pieced fabric square; draw around pattern. Do not cut out.
3. Referring to photo, fuse small heart to center of large heart. Follow **Almost Invisible Appliqué**, page 149, to stitch in place.
4. Follow **Quilting**, page 151, to layer and quilt in the ditch around small heart. Machine stitch through all layers on large heart outline. Cut $^{1}/_{8}$" outside stitching line.
5. To complete pillow with welting, follow **Pillow Finishing**, page 157, trimming seam allowance to $^{1}/_{4}$" after adding welting.
6. Cut one 12" length and two 10" lengths of ribbon. Tie each 10" ribbon into a bow. Refer to photo and sew each end of 12" ribbon to front of pillow to form a hanger. Sew 1 bow and 1 button at each end of hanger.
7. Refer to **Embroidery Stitches**, page 158, and to photo to add embroidery to pillow. Add beads as desired.

Happy Heart Pattern

Large Heart Pattern

Wall Hanging Heart Pattern

PATRIOTIC COLLECTION

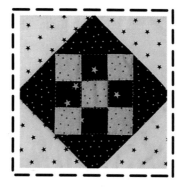

As American as apple pie, patriotic patchwork quilts were often designed to celebrate historical events — from presidential elections and Fourth of July festivities to centennial celebrations. You can create a star-spangled observance of your own with our red, white, and blue quilt and coordinating kitchen accessories. Our instructions, based on the timeworn Nine-Patch-in-a-Square quilt shown here, use rotary cutting and strip piecing to eliminate the need for templates — making a simple pattern even easier. And, working with fewer fabrics than our antique quilt makes assembling the basic nine-patch units as easy as pie!

Bursting with flag-waving spirit, these quilted kitchen accessories are great for serving apple pie — or any favorite dish! The handy pot holders are easy to assemble using Nine-Patch-in-a-Square blocks. And basic nine-patch blocks make perfectly cute coasters. This spangled table runner will fill your kitchen with stars and stripes. Its patriotic sentiments are embroidered with easy running stitches.

(Opposite) Featuring a charming quilt-block bib, this easy-to-stitch apron is a Yankee-Doodle dandy!

PATRIOTIC NINE-PATCH QUILT

SKILL LEVEL: 1 2 3 4 5
BLOCK SIZE: 5¼" x 5¼"
QUILT SIZE: 68" x 79"

Our antique scrap quilt features many blue and white prints. Our instructions for making a similar quilt using quick-method techniques use 6 different blue prints and 6 different white prints.

YARDAGE REQUIREMENTS
Yardage is based on 45"w fabric.

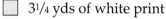 3¼ yds of white print

1⅜ yds of red

¼ yd **each** of 6 assorted dark blue prints

¼ yd **each** of 6 assorted white prints
5½ yds for backing
1 yd for binding
72" x 90" batting

CUTTING OUT THE PIECES
All measurements include a ¼" seam allowance. Follow Rotary Cutting, page 144, to cut fabric.

1. **From white print:**
   - Cut 2 lengthwise strips 5½" x 62" for **top/bottom borders**. Cut 2 lengthwise strips 5½" x 83" for **side borders**.
   - Cut 5¾"w strips from remaining fabric width. From these strips, cut a total of 71 squares 5¾" x 5¾" for **setting squares**.

setting square (cut 71)

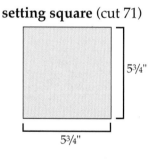

5¾"

5¾"

2. **From red:**
   - Cut 12 selvage-to-selvage strips 3½"w. From these strips, cut a total of 144 squares 3½" x 3½". Cut squares once diagonally to make 288 **triangles**.

square (cut 144)   **triangle** (cut 288)

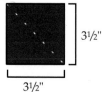

3½"

3½"

3. **From *each* of 6 blue prints:**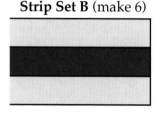
   - Cut 3 selvage-to-selvage **strips** 1¾"w.
4. **From *each* of 6 white prints:**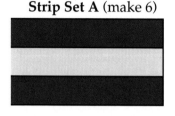
   - Cut 3 selvage-to-selvage **strips** 1¾"w.

ASSEMBLING THE QUILT TOP
Follow Piecing and Pressing, page 146, to make quilt top.

1. Choose 3 matching blue **strips** and 3 matching white **strips** to assemble **Strip Set A** and **Strip Set B** as shown. Make 6 **Strip Set A's** and 6 **Strip Set B's**.

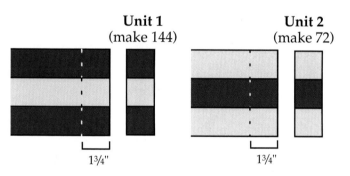

Strip Set A (make 6)   **Strip Set B** (make 6)

2. Cut across **Strip Set A's** and **Strip Set B's** at 1¾" intervals to make a total of 144 **Unit 1's** and 72 **Unit 2's**.

Unit 1
(make 144)   **Unit 2**
(make 72)

1¾"   1¾"

3. Assemble a matching set of 2 **Unit 1's** and 1 **Unit 2** as shown to make **Unit 3**. Make 72 **Unit 3's**.

Unit 3 (make 72)

4. Assemble 4 **triangles** and 1 **Unit 3** as shown to make **Block**. Make 72 **Blocks**.

Block (make 72)

5. Assemble **Blocks** and **setting squares** as shown to make **Row A** and **Row B**. Make 7 **Row A's** and 6 **Row B's**.

Row A (make 7)

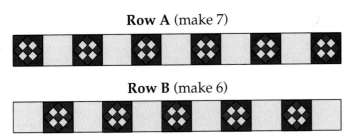

Row B (make 6)

6. Referring to **Quilt Top Diagram**, assemble **Rows** to complete center section of quilt top.
7. Follow **Adding Squared Borders**, page 150, and **Quilt Top Diagram** to add **top**, **bottom**, and then **side borders** to complete **Quilt Top**.

COMPLETING THE QUILT
1. Follow **Quilting**, page 151, and **Quilting Diagram** to mark, layer, and quilt.
2. Cut a 36" square of binding fabric. Follow **Making Continuous Bias Strip Binding**, page 155, to make approximately 10 yds of 2½"w bias binding.
3. Follow **Attaching Binding with Mitered Corners**, page 155, to attach binding to quilt.

Quilt Top Diagram

Quilting Diagram

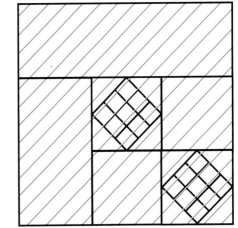

LIBERTY TABLE RUNNER

TABLE RUNNER SIZE: 21" x 60"

YARDAGE REQUIREMENTS
Yardage is based on 45"w fabric.

- ⬜ ⅝ yd of tan print
- ⬛ ⅝ yd of blue print
- ⬛ ⅜ yd of red print
- ⬛ ¼ yd of tan stripe
  1¾ yds for backing
  ¾ yd for binding
  24" x 63" batting

You will also need:
  blue embroidery floss

CUTTING OUT THE PIECES
All measurements include a ¼" seam allowance. Follow Rotary Cutting, page 144, to cut fabric.

1. **From tan print:** ⬜
   - Cut 3 selvage-to-selvage **strips** 1¾"w.
   - Cut 1 piece 14" x 38½" for **table runner center**.

2. **From blue print:** ⬛
   - Cut 8 selvage-to-selvage **strips** 1¾"w.
   - Cut 1 selvage-to-selvage **strip** 3½"w. From this strip, cut a total of 8 squares 3½" x 3½". Cut squares once diagonally to make 16 **triangles**.

square (cut 8)

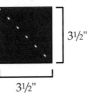

3½"

3½"

triangle (cut 16)

3. **From tan stripe:**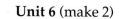
   - Cut 4 selvage-to-selvage **strips** 1³/₄"w.
4. **From red print:** ■
   - Cut 3 selvage-to-selvage **strips** 1³/₄"w.
   - Cut 2 selvage-to-selvage strips 1¹/₂"w. From these strips, cut a total of 4 **large rectangles** 1¹/₂" x 14".
   - Cut 1 selvage-to-selvage strip 1¹/₂"w. From this strip, cut a total of 6 **small rectangles** 1¹/₂" x 5³/₄".

ASSEMBLING TABLE RUNNER TOP

Follow **Piecing and Pressing**, *page 146, to make table runner top.*

1. Assemble **strips** as shown to make **Strip Set A** and **Strip Set B**. Cut across **Strip Set A** at 1³/₄" intervals to make a total of 14 **Unit 1's**. Cut across **Strip Set B** at 1³/₄" intervals to make a total of 16 **Unit 2's**.

Strip Set A (make 1)   **Unit 1** (cut 14)

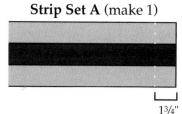

1³/₄"

Strip Set B (make 1)   **Unit 2** (cut 16)

1³/₄"

2. Assemble 2 **Unit 1's** and 1 **Unit 2** as shown to make **Unit 3**. Make 4 **Unit 3's**. Assemble 2 **Unit 2's** and 1 **Unit 1** as shown to make **Unit 4**. Make 6 **Unit 4's**.

Unit 3 (make 4)   **Unit 4** (make 6)

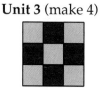

3. Assemble 4 **triangles** and 1 **Unit 3** as shown to make **Unit 5**. Make 4 **Unit 5's**.

Unit 5 (make 4)

4. Assemble 2 **Unit 5's**, 3 **small rectangles**, and 2 **large rectangles** as shown to make **Unit 6**. Make 2 **Unit 6's**.

Unit 6 (make 2)

5. Referring to **Table Runner Top Diagram**, assemble 2 **Unit 6's** and **table runner center** to complete center section of table runner top.
6. Assemble **strips** as shown to make **Strip Set C**. Make 4 **Strip Set C's**. Cut across **Strip Set C's** at 24⁵/₈" intervals to make a total of 4 **Border Unit A's**. Cut across remaining **Strip Set C** lengths at 14" intervals to make a total of 2 **Border Unit B's**.

Strip Set C (make 4)

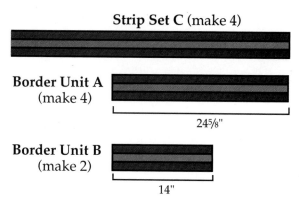

Border Unit A
(make 4)

24⁵/₈"

Border Unit B
(make 2)

14"

7. Assemble 3 **Unit 4's** and 2 **Border Unit A's** as shown to make **Unit 7**. Make 2 **Unit 7's**.

Unit 7 (make 2)

8. Referring to **Table Runner Top Diagram**, attach **Border Unit B's** to ends and **Unit 7's** to sides of center section of table runner top.
9. Referring to photo and **Table Runner Top Diagram**, mark words on **Table Runner Top**. Use 6 strands of floss and long running stitches to stitch along marked lines.

COMPLETING THE TABLE RUNNER

1. Referring to photo and arranging stars on table runner center as desired, use **Star Patterns**, page 43, and follow **Quilting**, page 151, to mark and layer table runner; quilt along marked lines and in the ditch along seamlines.

2. Cut a 27" square for binding. Follow **Making Continuous Bias Strip Binding**, page 155, to make approximately 4³/4 yds of 2¹/2"w bias binding.

3. Follow **Attaching Binding with Mitered Corners**, page 155, to attach binding to table runner.

Table Runner Top Diagram

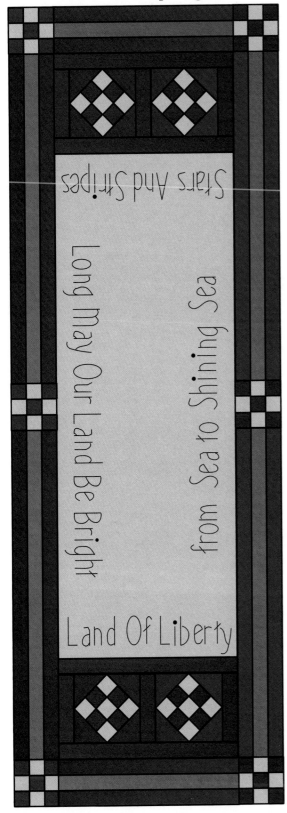

NINE-PATCH COASTERS

COASTER SIZE: 4¹/4" x 4¹/4"

Instructions are for making a set of 4 coasters.

YARDAGE REQUIREMENTS
Yardage is based on 45"w fabric.

- ■ ¹/4 yd of blue print
- □ ¹/4 yd of white print
  3/8 yd for backing
  2 yds of 1¹/2"w bias binding
  18" x 18" batting

CUTTING OUT THE PIECES
All measurements include a ¹/4" seam allowance. Follow **Rotary Cutting**, *page 144, to cut fabric.*

1. **From blue print:** ■
   - Cut **3 strips** 1³/4" x 20".
2. **From white print:** □
   - Cut **3 strips** 1³/4" x 20".

MAKING THE COASTERS
Follow **Piecing and Pressing**, *page 146, to make coasters.*

1. Assemble **strips** as shown to make **Strip Set A** and **Strip Set B**. Cut across **Strip Set A** at 1³/4" intervals to make a total of 8 **Unit 1's**. Cut across **Strip Set B** at 1³/4" intervals to make a total of 4 **Unit 2's**.

Strip Set A (make 1)   **Unit 1** (make 8)

1³/4"

Strip Set B (make 1)   **Unit 2** (make 4)

1³/4"

2. Assemble 2 **Unit 1's** and 1 **Unit 2** as shown to make **Coaster Top**. Make 4 **Coaster Tops**.

Coaster Top (make 4)

3. Cut batting and backing fabric into 4 squares 9" x 9". Follow **Quilting**, page 151, to layer and quilt each coaster in the ditch along seamlines.

4. Cut bias binding into 4 equal lengths and follow **Attaching Binding with Mitered Corners**, page 155, to attach binding to each coaster.

PATRIOTIC APRON

YARDAGE REQUIREMENTS

Yardage is based on 45"w fabric.

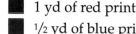 1 yd of red print

 1/2 yd of blue print

3/8 yd of tan stripe

scrap of tan print
13" x 13" square for backing
13" x 13" square of batting

CUTTING OUT THE PIECES

All measurements include a 1/4" seam allowance. Follow **Rotary Cutting**, *page 144, to cut fabric.*

1. **From red print:**

   • Cut 1 piece 25½" x 35" for **skirt**.
   • Cut 2 squares 4½" x 4½". Cut squares once diagonally to make 4 **triangles**.

   square (cut 2)   **triangle** (cut 4)

     4½"
   4½"

   • Cut 4 **squares** 1¾" x 1¾".

2. **From blue print:**

   • Cut 2 squares 3½" x 3½". Cut squares once diagonally to make 4 **triangles**.

   square (cut 2)   **triangle** (cut 4)

   3½"
   3½"

   • Cut 2 pieces 5" x 35¼" for **waistband**.

3. **From tan stripe:**

   • Cut 2 pieces 1¾" x 8" for **side borders**.
   • Cut 2 pieces 1¾" x 10½" for **top/bottom borders**.
   • Cut 2 pieces 3¼" x 28" for **neck ties**.

4. **From tan print:**

   • Cut 5 **squares** 1¾" x 1¾".

MAKING THE APRON

Follow **Piecing and Pressing**, *page 146, to make apron.*

1. Assemble **squares** as shown to make **Unit 1**.

Unit 1 (make 1)

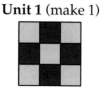

2. Assemble **triangles** and **Unit 1** as shown to make **Unit 2**.

Unit 2 (make 1)

3. Assemble **triangles** and **Unit 2** as shown to make **Unit 3**.

Unit 3 (make 1)

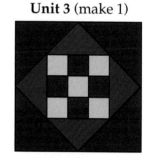

4. Attach **side**, then **top** and **bottom borders** to **Unit 3** to complete **Block**.

Block

5. Layer **Block** and backing with right sides together on top of batting. Leaving bottom edge open, sew all layers together. Trim batting close to seam allowance. Turn right side out and press.

6. Follow **Quilting**, page 151, and quilt in the ditch along seamlines.

7. Press each short edge and 1 long edge of **skirt** 1/2" to wrong side; press 1/2" to wrong side again and stitch in place. Baste 1/2" and 1/4" from raw edge (top). Pull basting threads, drawing up gathers to measure 17".

8. Sew short edges of **waistband** pieces together to make 1 piece. Press all edges of **waistband** 1/2" to wrong side. With wrong sides together, press **waistband** in half lengthwise.

9. Centering **skirt** on **waistband**, insert gathered edge of skirt 1/2" between pressed edges of **waistband**; pin in place. Beginning at 1 end of **waistband**, topstitch close to pressed edges.

10. Place **Block** and **waistband** right sides up. With **Block** centered, overlap top edge of **waistband** 1/4" over bottom edge of **Block**. Stitching close to top edge of **waistband**, sew **Block** to **waistband**.

11. Press 1 short edge of each **neck tie** 1/2" to wrong side. Matching right sides, fold in half lengthwise. Sew along short and long raw edges, leaving pressed short edge open for turning. Turn right side out; press. Blindstitch opening closed.

12. Blindstitch 1 **neck tie** to each top corner on wrong side of **Block** to complete **Apron**.

PATRIOTIC POT HOLDERS

POT HOLDER SIZE: 8" x 8"

Instructions are for making 1 pot holder.

YARDAGE REQUIREMENTS
Yardage is based on 45"w fabric.

 1 fat quarter (18" x 22" piece) **each** of tan print, red print, blue print, and white print
10" x 10" square for backing
1 yd of 1 1/2"w bias binding
10" x 10" square of batting

CUTTING OUT THE PIECES
All measurements include a 1/4" seam allowance. Follow Rotary Cutting, page 144, to cut fabric.

1. **From tan print:** ◻
   • Cut 5 **squares** 1 3/4" x 1 3/4".

2. **From red print:** ◼
   • Cut 4 **squares** 1 3/4" x 1 3/4".

3. **From blue print:** ◼
   • Cut 2 squares 3 1/2" x 3 1/2". Cut squares once diagonally to make 4 **triangles**.

square (cut 2)   **triangle** (cut 4)

3 1/2"

3 1/2"

• Cut 1 piece 2" x 6 1/2" for **hanging loop**.

4. **From white print:** ◻
   • Cut 2 squares 4 1/2" x 4 1/2". Cut squares once diagonally to make 4 **triangles**.

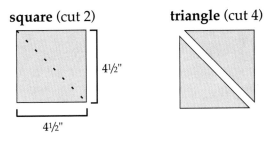

square (cut 2)   **triangle** (cut 4)

4 1/2"

4 1/2"

MAKING THE POT HOLDER
Follow Piecing and Pressing, page 146, to make pot holder.

1. Referring to **Pot Holder Top** diagram, follow Steps 1 - 3 of **Making the Apron** for **Patriotic Apron**, page 42, to make **Pot Holder Top**.

Pot Holder Top

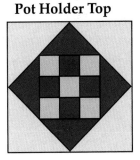

2. Follow **Quilting**, page 151, to layer and quilt in the ditch along seamlines.

3. Follow **Attaching Binding with Mitered Corners**, page 155, to attach binding to pot holder.

4. Press all edges of **hanging loop** 1/2" to wrong side. With wrong sides together, press hanging loop in half lengthwise; sew close to pressed edges. Matching ends, fold in half to form loop. Blindstitch ends of hanging loop to 1 corner on back of pot holder.

Star Patterns

LONE STAR

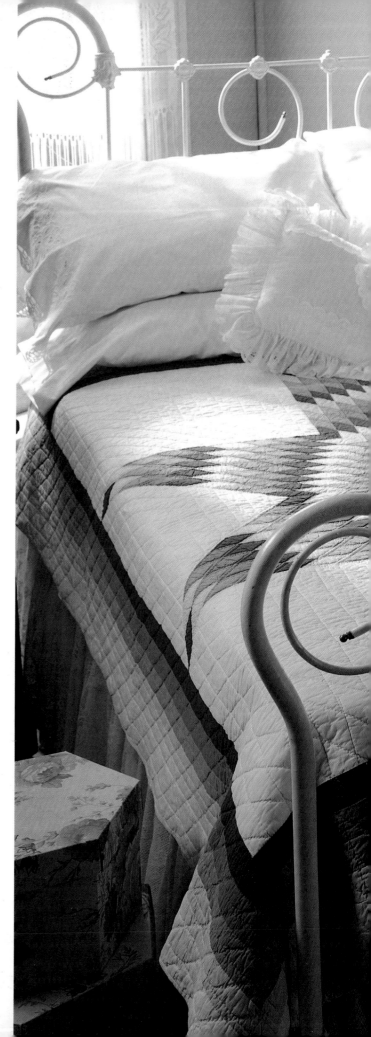

Star patterns have long been favorites among quilters, and the dramatic Lone Star is one of the most challenging. Also known as the Star of Bethlehem, the design covers the whole quilt top — typical of a style popular in the 1800's. To simplify this advanced quilt, we strip pieced the fabrics and then cut them diagonally to create the rows of diamonds for the star. A rainbow of stripes forms a dramatic, easy border.

LONE STAR QUILT

SKILL LEVEL: 1 2 3 4 5
QUILT SIZE: 82" x 82"

YARDAGE REQUIREMENTS

Yardage is based on 45"w fabric.

☐ 3¼ yds of white
◻ 2¾ yds of light pink
◻ 2¾ yds of pink
◼ 2¾ yds of purple
■ 2¾ yds of blue
7 yds for backing
1 yd for binding
90" x 108" batting

CUTTING OUT THE PIECES

All measurements include a ¼" seam allowance. Follow
Rotary Cutting, page 144, to cut fabric.

1. **From white:** ☐
   - Cut 4 lengthwise strips 4" x 89" for **borders**.
   - Cut 4 squares 19³/₄" x 19³/₄" for **corner squares**.

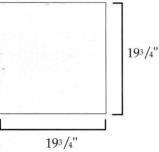

corner square (cut 4)

19³/₄"

19³/₄"

   - Cut 1 square 28¹/₄" x 28¹/₄". Cut square twice diagonally to make 4 **side triangles**.

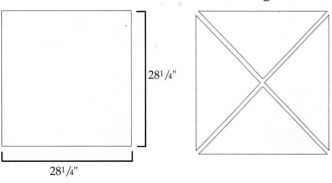

side triangle (cut 4)

28¹/₄"

28¹/₄"

2. **From light pink:**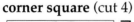
   - Cut 4 lengthwise strips 2" x 89" for **borders**.
   - Cut 20 **strips** 2"w x remaining fabric width.

3. **From pink:** ◻
   - Cut 4 lengthwise strips 2" x 89" for **borders**.
   - Cut 20 **strips** 2"w x remaining fabric width.

4. **From purple:** ◼
   - Cut 4 lengthwise strips 2" x 89" for **borders**.
   - Cut 20 **strips** 2"w x remaining fabric width.

5. **From blue:** ■
   - Cut 4 lengthwise strips 2" x 89" for **borders**.
   - Cut 21 **strips** 2"w x remaining fabric width.

ASSEMBLING THE QUILT TOP

Follow Piecing and Pressing, page 146, to make quilt top.

1. Assemble each strip set in the color order shown, adding each new **strip** 1½" from the end of the previous strip to make **Strip Sets A, B, C,** and **D**. Make 3 **Strip Set A's** and 2 each of **Strip Sets B, C,** and **D**.

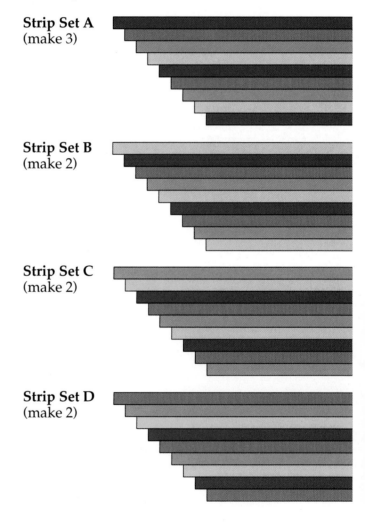

Strip Set A
(make 3)

Strip Set B
(make 2)

Strip Set C
(make 2)

Strip Set D
(make 2)

2. Referring to **Fig. 1**, use a large right-angle triangle aligned with a seam to determine an accurate 45° cutting line. Use rotary cutter and rotary cutting ruler to trim the uneven ends from one end of each **Strip Set**.

Fig. 1

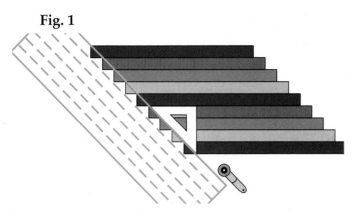

3. Aligning the 45° mark on the rotary cutting ruler (shown in pink) with a seam and aligning the 2" mark with the edge of the cut made in Step 2, cut across **Strip Sets** at 2" intervals as shown in **Fig. 2**.

Fig. 2

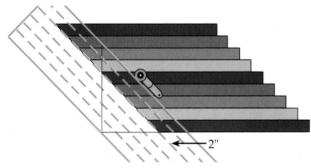

From **Strip Set A's**, cut a total of 24 **Unit 1's**.

Unit 1 (cut 24)

From **Strip Set B's**, cut a total of 16 **Unit 2's**.

Unit 2 (cut 16)

From **Strip Set C's**, cut a total of 16 **Unit 3's**.

Unit 3 (cut 16)

From **Strip Set D's**, cut a total of 16 **Unit 4's**.

Unit 4 (cut 16)

4. When making **Unit 5's**, refer to **Fig. 3** to match long edges of units. Seams will cross 1/4" from cut edges of fabric. Pin and stitch as shown in **Fig. 3**. Assemble 3 **Unit 1's**, 2 **Unit 2's**, 2 **Unit 3's**, and 2 **Unit 4's** in order shown to make **Unit 5**. Make 8 **Unit 5's**.

Fig. 3

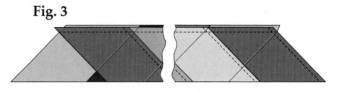

Unit 5 (make 8)

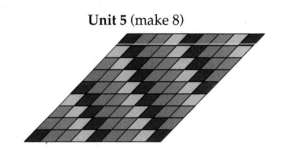

5. To make **Unit 6**, place 2 **Unit 5's** right sides together, carefully matching edges and seams; pin. Stitch in direction shown in **Fig. 4**, ending stitching 1/4" from edge of fabric (you may find it helpful to mark a small dot at this point before sewing) and backstitching at end of seam. Make 4 **Unit 6's**.

Fig. 4

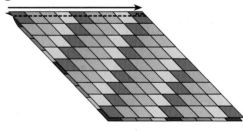

Unit 6 (make 4)

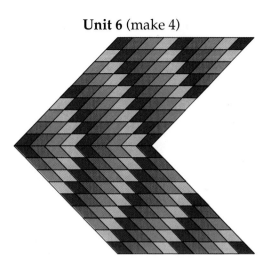

6. Referring to **Quilt Top Diagram**, assemble **Unit 6's** to make **Star**, always ending stitching 1/4" from edges and backstitching.
7. Follow **Working With Diamond Shapes**, page 147, to attach **corner squares**, then **side triangles**, to Star to complete center section of quilt top as shown in **Quilt Top Diagram**.

8. Assemble **borders** as shown to make **Border Unit**. Make 4 **Border Units**.

Border Unit (make 4)

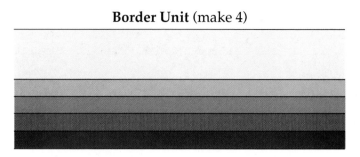

9. Follow **Adding Mitered Borders**, page 150, and attach **Border Units** to complete **Quilt Top**.

COMPLETING THE QUILT
1. Follow **Quilting**, page 151, and **Quilting Diagram** to mark, layer, and quilt.
2. Cut a 36" square of fabric for binding. Follow **Making Continuous Bias Strip Binding**, page 155, to make approximately 10 yds of 2 1/2"w bias binding.
3. Follow **Attaching Binding with Mitered Corners**, page 155, to attach binding to quilt.

Quilting Diagram

AMISH COLLECTION

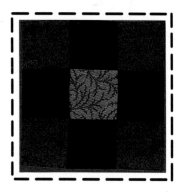

No other people are more renowned for masterful quilting than the Amish communities of Ohio, Pennsylvania, and Indiana. Remarkably, the Amish didn't begin quilting until the late 1800's when they were influenced by their contemporary neighbors to turn away from traditional woven coverlets. Each Amish community soon developed its individual quilting style, but all followed a custom of humility by piecing solid fabrics in simple patterns. The Chinese Coins quilt shown here was made by Amish craftswomen in Ohio. To create a similar quilt, simply rotary cut long strips of fabric, piece them together into a rectangle, and cut the rectangle into columns that stack together for quick assembly. Any color combination will work with this random scheme of hues, and the large solid areas provide a showcase for beautiful quilting.

The rich tones and bold patterns of traditional Amish quilts also look wonderful on home decorations and clothing. We used a simple Nine-Patch variation pattern (below) to embellish our black sweatshirt. (Opposite) You can add a dramatic accent to your decor with a Chinese Coins wall hanging similar to this one. It features the same striking colors and elegant stitching as our large quilt, but the small size lets you finish in a fraction of the time!

CHINESE COINS QUILT

SKILL LEVEL: 1 2 3 4 5
QUILT SIZE: 68" x 81"

YARDAGE REQUIREMENTS
Yardage is based on 45"w fabric.

 4½ yds of black

2 yds **total** of assorted solids (our quilt uses 19 different solids)
5 yds for backing
⅝ yd for binding
81" x 96" batting

CUTTING OUT THE PIECES
All measurements include a ¼" seam allowance. Follow Rotary Cutting, page 144, to cut fabric.

1. **From black:**
    - Cut 5 lengthwise strips 6" x 61½" for **sashing strips**.
    - Cut 2 lengthwise strips 8" x 56½" for **top/bottom outer borders**.
    - Cut 2 lengthwise strips 8" x 85" for **side outer borders**.

2. **From assorted solids:**
    - Cut 1 or more selvage-to-selvage **strips** from each fabric in widths varying from 1½"w to 2¼"w.

ASSEMBLING THE QUILT TOP
Follow Piecing and Pressing, page 146, to make quilt top. Assemble strips and units in random fabric combinations.

1. Assemble **strips** as shown to make a **Strip Set** 21½"l. Make 3 **Strip Sets**. Cut across **Strip Sets** at 5½" intervals to make a total of 12 **Unit 1's**. Cut across remaining **Strip Sets** at 2¾" intervals to make a total of 12 **Unit 2's**.

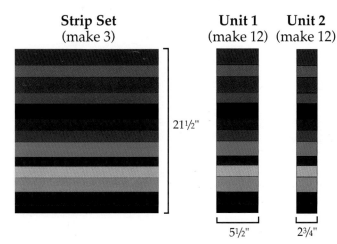

Strip Set (make 3)   **Unit 1** (make 12)   **Unit 2** (make 12)

21½"

5½"   2¾"

2. Sew short edges of all **Unit 1's** together to make 1 **Pieced Strip**. Cut across **Pieced Strip** at 61½" intervals to make a total of 4 **Unit 3's**.

Unit 3 (make 4)

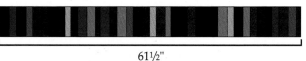

61½"

3. Referring to **Quilt Top Diagram**, assemble **Unit 3's** and **sashing strips** to complete center section of quilt top.

4. Sew short edges of all **Unit 2's** together to make 1 **Border Strip**. Cut across **Border Strip** at 48" intervals to make 2 **top/bottom inner borders**. Cut across remainder of **Border Strip** at 66" intervals to make 2 **side inner borders**.

Border Strip (make 1)

5. Follow **Adding Squared Borders**, page 150, and **Quilt Top Diagram** and attach **top, bottom**, and then **side inner borders** to center section of quilt top. Add **top, bottom**, and then **side outer borders** to complete **Quilt Top**.

COMPLETING THE QUILT

1. Follow **Quilting**, page 151, **Quilting Diagram**, **Feather Template Pattern**, and **Cable Pattern**, page 57, to mark, layer, and quilt. To mark feather pattern, refer to placement line on **Quilt Top Diagram** and follow Step 3 of **Using Quilting Stencils and Templates**, page 152.
2. Follow **Making Straight-Grain Binding**, page 155, to make 2½"w straight-grain binding.
3. Follow **Attaching Binding with Overlapped Corners**, page 156, to attach binding to quilt.

Feather Template Pattern

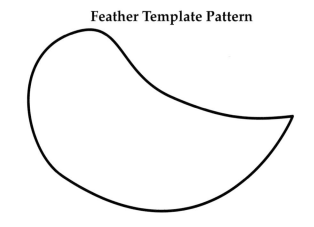

Quilt Top Diagram

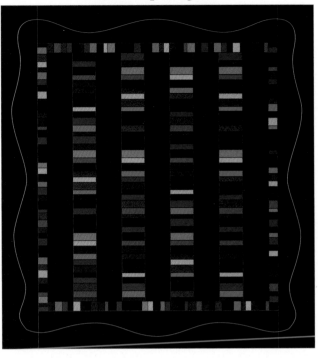

Blue line indicates placement line for feather quilting pattern.

Quilting Diagram

AMISH SWEATSHIRT

YARDAGE REQUIREMENTS

Yardage is based on 45"w fabric.

$1/8$ yd of blue
$1/8$ yd of magenta
$1/8$ yd of teal
scraps of teal print, black, purple print, and
light purple print

You will also need:
a black sweatshirt with set-in sleeves
paper-backed fusible web

MAKING THE SWEATSHIRT

*All measurements include a $1/4$" seam allowance. Refer to photo and follow **Piecing and Pressing**, page 146, to make sweatshirt.*

1. Wash, dry, and press sweatshirt and fabrics.
2. Measure front of sweatshirt from armhole to armhole $4^1/2$" below neck band (**Fig. 1**); add 6". Cut one 2"w strip each the determined measurement from blue, magenta, and teal.

Fig. 1

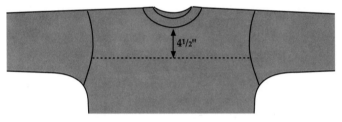

3. Sew long edges of strips together to make a single strip. Press long raw edges of strip $1/4$" to wrong side.
4. Center strip across front of sweatshirt with top long edge $4^1/2$" below neck band; pin in place. Use seam ripper to open armhole seams as far as necessary to insert ends of strip into shirt at seams.
5. Topstitch along seams and pressed edges of strip on sweatshirt front. Trim short edges of strip even with raw edges of armholes.
6. Cut the following squares $2^1/2$" x $2^1/2$": 1 from teal print, 4 from black, and 4 from purple print.
7. Assemble squares to make a nine-patch block.
8. From light purple print, cut 2 pieces $1^1/4$" x $6^1/2$" for side borders and 2 pieces $1^1/4$" x 8" for top and bottom borders. Attach side, then top and bottom borders to block.
9. Press borders $3/4$" to wrong side. Cut a square $6^1/4$" x $6^1/4$" of web. Fuse web to center of wrong side of block. Remove paper backing.
10. Fuse block to sweatshirt front over strip.
11. Topstitch along pressed edges of borders.
12. Turn shirt wrong side out and stitch armhole seams closed along previous seamlines.

CHINESE COINS WALL HANGING

SKILL LEVEL: 1 2 3 4 5
WALL HANGING SIZE: 37" x 41"

YARDAGE REQUIREMENTS
Yardage is based on 45"w fabric.

- 1¹⁄₈ yds of black
- 1¹⁄₂ yds **total** of assorted solids (our wall hanging uses 19 different solids)
- ¹⁄₄ yd desired solid for inner borders
  1¹⁄₂ yds for backing and hanging sleeve
  ¹⁄₂ yd for binding
  40" x 45" batting

CUTTING OUT THE PIECES
All measurements include a ¹⁄₄" seam allowance. Follow Rotary Cutting, page 144, to cut fabric.

1. **From black:**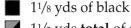
   - Cut 4 selvage-to-selvage strips 2³⁄₄" w. From these strips, cut 4 pieces 2³⁄₄" x 26" for **sashing strips**.
   - Cut 2 selvage-to-selvage strips 5¹⁄₂"w. From these strips, cut 2 pieces 5¹⁄₂" x 26¹⁄₂" for **top/bottom outer borders**.
   - Cut 2 selvage-to-selvage strips 5¹⁄₂"w. From these strips, cut 2 pieces 5¹⁄₂" x 40¹⁄₂" for **side outer borders**.

2. **From assorted solids:**
   - Cut 1 or more 20"l **strips** from each fabric in widths varying from 1¹⁄₄"w to 1³⁄₄"w.

3. **From desired solid for inner border:**
   - Cut 2 selvage-to-selvage strips 2¹⁄₄"w. From these strips, cut 2 pieces 2¹⁄₄" x 22" for **top/bottom inner borders**.
   - Cut 2 selvage-to-selvage strips 2¹⁄₄"w. From these strips, cut 2 pieces 2¹⁄₄" x 30¹⁄₂" for **side inner borders**.

ASSEMBLING THE WALL HANGING TOP
Follow Piecing and Pressing, page 146, to make wall hanging top.

1. Assemble **strips** randomly as shown to make a **Strip Set** 26"l. Cut across **Strip Set** at 3" intervals to make a total of 5 **Unit 1's**.

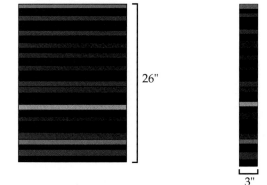

Strip Set (make 1)   **Unit 1** (make 5)

26"   3"

2. Referring to **Wall Hanging Top Diagram**, assemble **Unit 1's** and **Sashing Strips** as shown to complete center section of wall hanging top.
3. Follow **Adding Squared Borders**, page 150, and **Wall Hanging Top Diagram** to attach **top**, **bottom**, and then **side inner borders**. Add **top**, **bottom**, and then **side outer borders** to complete **Wall Hanging Top**.

COMPLETING THE WALL HANGING

1. Follow **Quilting**, page 151, **Quilting Diagram**, and **Leaf** and **Scallop Patterns** to mark, layer, and quilt.
2. Follow **Making a Hanging Sleeve**, page 157, to attach hanging sleeve to wall hanging.
3. Follow **Making Straight-Grain Binding**, page 155, to make 2¹⁄₂"w straight-grain binding.
4. Follow **Attaching Binding with Overlapped Corners**, page 156, to attach binding to wall hanging.

Wall Hanging Top Diagram

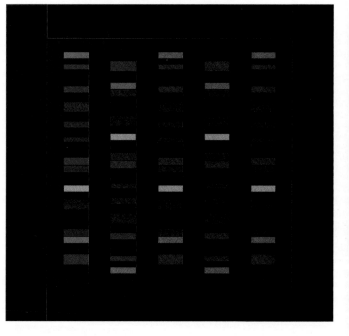

Quilting Diagram

Leaf Pattern

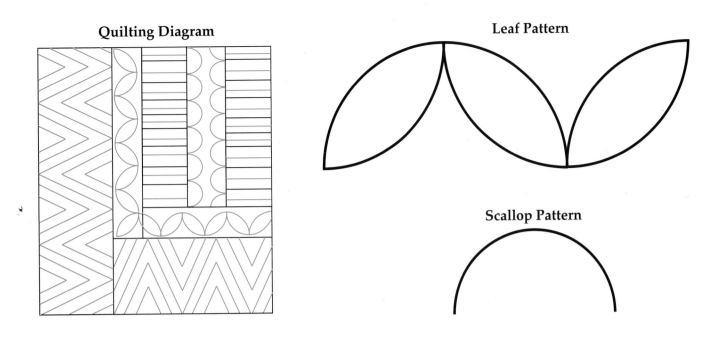

Scallop Pattern

Cable Pattern

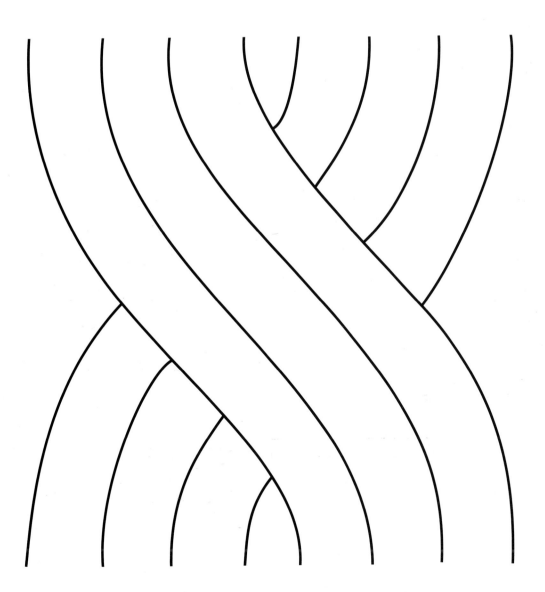

SPRING BASKET COLLECTION

As pretty as they are practical, baskets have always inspired quiltmakers. Not until the Civil War era, however, did basket designs emerge in pieced patchwork blocks rather than appliqué. To bring out the feminine beauty of our Spring Basket quilt, we used a gardenful of soft pastels and floral prints. We made sewing the blocks much simpler than the traditional approach by rotary cutting all the fabrics and strip piecing many of the units. Working with large fabric pieces in the setting blocks and borders makes piecing the top even faster!

Any stitcher will be delighted with the combination of floral and grid quilting that adds a fresh finishing touch to this beauty.

The dainty floral prints and other pastel fabrics used in our collection are perfect for a young girl's bedroom! She'll love the coordinating pillows and wall hanging, which are made with the same fabrics found in our Spring Basket quilt. The frilly — and fast — patchwork throw pillow is super-simple to stitch using colorful scraps. Just rotary cut the pieces into squares, strip piece them together, and add a gingham ruffle for a delightful finish. (Opposite) Edged with a scrapwork border, this wall hanging blooms to life with a Spring Basket quilt block, elegant quilting, and appliquéd blossoms cut from print fabrics.

SPRING BASKET QUILT

SKILL LEVEL: 1 2 3 4 5
BLOCK SIZE: 10½" x 10½"
QUILT SIZE: 81" x 95"

YARDAGE REQUIREMENTS
Yardage is based on 45"w fabric.

- 3¼ yds of large yellow print
- 2⅝ yds of floral with blue background
- 2⅝ yds of pink check
- 1¾ yds of white print
- ⅝ yd of green print
- ⅜ yd of pink print
- ⅜ yd of small yellow print
- 7½ yds for backing
- 1 yd for binding
- 90" x 108" batting

CUTTING OUT THE PIECES
All measurements include a ¼" seam allowance. Follow Rotary Cutting, page 144, to cut fabric.

1. **From large yellow print:**
   - Cut 2 strips 8½" x 99" for **side outer borders**.
   - Cut 2 strips 8½" x 68" for **top/bottom outer borders**.
   - Cut 4 selvage-to-selvage **strips** 2¼"w.

2. **From floral with blue background:**
   - Cut 4 selvage-to-selvage strips 11"w. From these strips, cut 12 **setting squares** 11" x 11".
   - Cut 2 selvage-to-selvage strips 16⅛"w. From these strips, cut 4 squares 16⅛" x 16⅛". Cut squares twice diagonally to make 16 **side setting triangles** (you will need 14 and have 2 left over).

side setting triangle (cut 16)

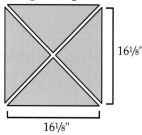

- Cut 2 squares 8¼" x 8¼". Cut squares once diagonally to make 4 **corner setting triangles**.

corner setting triangle (cut 4)

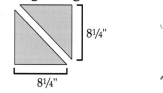

3. **From pink check:**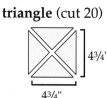
   - Cut 2 strips 2½" x 82" for **side inner borders**.
   - Cut 2 strips 2½" x 64" for **top/bottom inner borders**.
   - Cut 4 selvage-to-selvage **strips** 2¼"w.

4. **From white print:**
   - Cut 8 selvage-to-selvage strips 4"w. From these strips, cut 40 **small rectangles** 4" x 7½".
   - Cut 2 selvage-to-selvage strips 4"w. From these strips, cut 20 **squares** 4" x 4".
   - Cut 1 selvage-to-selvage strip 4¾"w. From this strip, cut 5 squares 4¾" x 4¾". Cut squares twice diagonally to make 20 **triangles**.

triangle (cut 20)

- Cut 1 **large rectangle** 10" x 23" for triangle-squares.

5. **From green print:**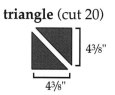
   - Cut 2 selvage-to-selvage strips 4⅜"w. From these strips, cut 10 squares 4⅜" x 4⅜". Cut squares once diagonally to make 20 **triangles**.

triangle (cut 20)

- Cut 1 **large rectangle** 10" x 23" for triangle-squares.

6. **From pink print:**
   - Cut 4 selvage-to-selvage **strips** 2¼"w.

7. **From small yellow print:**
   - Cut 4 selvage-to-selvage **strips** 2¼"w.

ASSEMBLING THE QUILT TOP
Follow Piecing and Pressing, page 146, to make quilt top.

1. To make triangle-squares, place green and white **large rectangles** right sides together. Referring to **Fig. 1**, follow Steps 1 - 3 of **Making Triangle-Squares**, page 146, to draw a grid of 10 squares 4⅜" x 4⅜". Referring to **Fig. 2** for sewing directions, follow Steps 4 - 6 of **Making Triangle-Squares**, page 146, to make a total of 20 **triangle-squares**.

Fig. 1

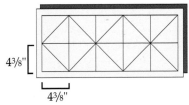

4³⁄₈"

4³⁄₈"

Fig. 2

triangle-square (make 20)

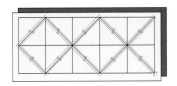

2. To cut parallelograms, refer to **Fig. 3** and place 2 matching **strips** right sides together on mat. Align the 45° marking on the rotary cutting ruler (shown in pink) along lower right edge of strips. Cut along right side of ruler to cut 1 end of both strips at a 45° angle.

Fig. 3

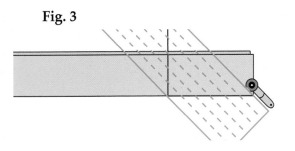

3. Turn cut strips 180° on mat and align the 45° marking on the rotary cutting ruler along lower left edge of strip. Align the previously cut 45° edge at the 3" marking on the ruler. Cut strips at 3" intervals as shown in **Fig 4**.

Fig. 4

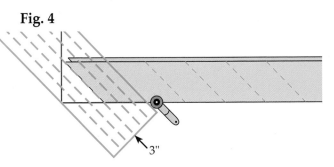

3"

4. Repeat Steps 2 and 3 with remaining **strips** to cut a total of 20 parallelograms each from large yellow print, pink check, pink print, and small yellow print.

5. Follow Step 1 of **Working with Diamond Shapes**, page 147, to assemble parallelograms to make 10 each of **Unit 1a**, **Unit 1b**, **Unit 1c**, and **Unit 1d**. Assemble **Units 1a, 1b, 1c,** and **1d** as shown to make 4 each of **Unit 2a** and **Unit 2d**; make 6 each of **Unit 2b** and **Unit 2c**. (*Note:* In remaining steps, **Unit 2a** will represent all **Unit 2** combinations.)

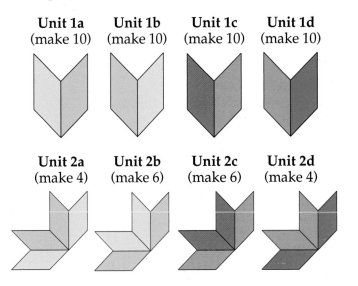

Unit 1a (make 10) **Unit 1b** (make 10) **Unit 1c** (make 10) **Unit 1d** (make 10)

Unit 2a (make 4) **Unit 2b** (make 6) **Unit 2c** (make 6) **Unit 2d** (make 4)

6. Follow Steps 2 and 3 of **Working with Diamond Shapes**, page 147, to assemble 1 **square** and 1 **Unit 2** as shown to make **Unit 3**. Make 20 **Unit 3's**. Assemble 2 **triangles** and 1 **Unit 3** as shown to make **Unit 4**. Make 20 **Unit 4's**.

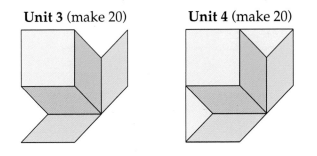

Unit 3 (make 20) **Unit 4** (make 20)

7. Assemble 1 **Unit 4** and 1 **triangle** as shown to make **Unit 5**. Make 20 **Unit 5's**.

Unit 5 (make 20)

8. Assemble 1 **Unit 5** and 1 **small rectangle** as shown to make **Unit 6**. Make 20 **Unit 6's**.

Unit 6 (make 20)

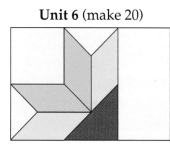

9. Assemble 1 **small rectangle** and 1 **triangle-square** as shown to make **Unit 7**. Make 20 **Unit 7's**.

Unit 7 (make 20)

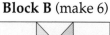

10. Assemble 1 **Unit 6** and 1 **Unit 7** as shown to make **Block**. Make 4 each of **Block A** and **Block D**; make 6 each of **Block B** and **Block C**.

Block A (make 4)

Block B (make 6)

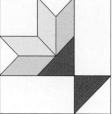

Block C (make 6)

Block D (make 4)

11. Refer to **Assembly Diagram** to assemble **Blocks**, **setting squares**, **side setting triangles**, and **corner setting triangles** into rows; sew rows together to complete center section of quilt top.

12. Follow **Adding Squared Borders**, page 150, and **Quilt Top Diagram** to add **top**, **bottom**, and then **side inner borders**. Add **top**, **bottom**, and then **side outer borders** to complete **Quilt Top**.

COMPLETING THE QUILT

1. Follow **Quilting**, page 151, and **Quilting Diagram** and use **Flower** and **Serpentine Quilting Patterns**, page 67, to mark, layer, and quilt.
2. Cut a 36" square of binding fabric. Follow **Making Continuous Bias Strip Binding**, page 155, to make approximately 10½ yds of 2½"w bias binding.
3. Follow **Attaching Binding with Mitered Corners**, page 155, to attach binding to quilt.

Assembly Diagram

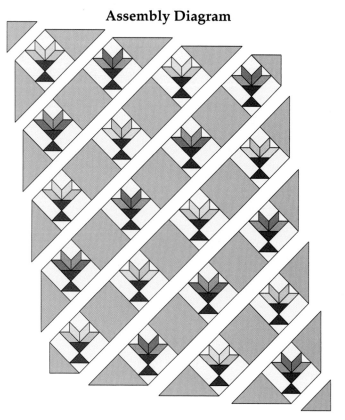

Quilting Diagram

Quilt Top Diagram

SPRING BASKET WALL HANGING

SKILL LEVEL: 1 2 3 4 5
WALL HANGING SIZE: 23" x 23"

YARDAGE REQUIREMENTS

Yardage is based on 45"w fabric.

- ☐ ³/₈ yd of white print
- ▦ ¹/₄ yd of floral with blue background
- ◩ 1 fat quarter (18" x 22" piece) **each** of green print, pink print, pink check, large yellow print, small yellow print, and floral with white background
- ■ ¹/₄ yd of green check for border
  floral scraps for appliqués
  1 yd for backing and hanging sleeve
  ¹/₂ yd for binding
  27" x 27" batting

You will also need:
  paper-backed fusible web
  transparent monofilament thread for appliqué

CUTTING OUT THE PIECES

All measurements include a ¹/₄" seam allowance. Follow Rotary Cutting, page 144, to cut fabric.

1. **From white print:**
   - Cut 2 **rectangles** 4" x 7¹/₂".
   - Cut 1 **square** 4" x 4".

- Cut 1 square 4³/₈" x 4³/₈". Cut square once diagonally to make a total of 2 **medium triangles** (you will need 1 and have 1 left over).

medium triangle (cut 2)

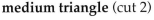

- Cut 2 squares 8¹/₄" x 8¹/₄". Cut each square once diagonally to make a total of 4 **large triangles**.

large triangle (cut 4)

- Cut 1 square 4³/₄" x 4³/₄". Cut square twice diagonally to make a total of 4 **small triangles** (you will need 2 and have 2 left over).

small triangle (cut 4)

2. **From floral with blue background:**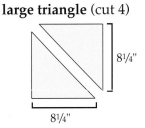
   - Cut 1 selvage-to-selvage strip 3¹/₂"w. From this strip, cut 4 **rectangles** 3¹/₂" x 4³/₈" and 4 **squares** 3¹/₂" x 3¹/₂".

3. **From green print:**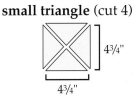
   - Cut 1 square 4³/₈" x 4³/₈". Cut square once diagonally to make a total of 2 **medium triangles**.

medium triangle (cut 2)

   - Cut 4 **squares** 3¹/₂" x 3¹/₂".

4. **From pink print:**
   - Cut 3 **squares** 3¹/₂" x 3¹/₂".

5. **From pink check:**
   - Cut 4 **squares** 3¹/₂" x 3¹/₂".
6. **From large yellow print:**
   - Cut 2 **rectangles** 2¹/₄" x 7".
   - Cut 2 **squares** 3¹/₂" x 3¹/₂".
7. **From small yellow print:**
   - Cut 2 **rectangles** 2¹/₄" x 7".
   - Cut 1 **square** 3¹/₂" x 3¹/₂".
8. **From floral with white background:**
   - Cut 2 **squares** 3¹/₂" x 3¹/₂".
9. **From green check:**
   - Cut 2 **strips** 1" x 15³/₈" for **top/bottom inner borders**.
   - Cut 2 **strips** 1" x 16³/₈" for **side borders**.

ASSEMBLING THE WALL HANGING TOP

Follow ***Piecing and Pressing***, *page 146, to make wall hanging top.*

1. Assemble 2 **medium triangles** as shown to make 1 **triangle-square**.

triangle-square (make 1)

2. Place large yellow print **rectangles** right sides together and follow Steps 2 and 3 of **Assembling the Quilt Top** for **Spring Basket Quilt**, page 63, to cut 1 parallelogram from each rectangle. Repeat for small yellow print **rectangles**.
3. Follow Steps 5 - 10 of **Assembling the Quilt Top** for **Spring Basket Quilt**, page 63, to make 1 **Block A**.

Block A (make 1)

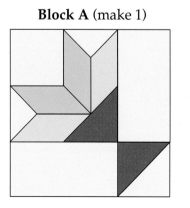

4. Referring to **Wall Hanging Top Diagram**, assemble **large triangles** and **Block A** to complete center section of wall hanging top.

5. Referring to **Wall Hanging Top Diagram**, attach **top**, **bottom**, and then **side inner borders** to center section of wall hanging top.
6. With floral with blue background rectangle placed at center of border, assemble 4 **squares** and 1 **rectangle** as shown to make 1 **Top Pieced Border** and 1 **Bottom Pieced Border**.

Top Pieced Border

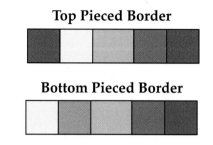

Bottom Pieced Border

7. With floral with blue background rectangle placed at center of border, assemble 6 **squares** and 1 **rectangle** as shown to make 1 **Right Pieced Border** and 1 **Left Pieced Border**.

Right Side Pieced Border

Left Side Pieced Border

8. Attach **Top**, **Bottom**, **Right**, and then **Left Pieced Borders** to center section of wall hanging top.
9. For appliqués, fuse web to wrong side of floral scraps. Cut desired motifs from fabric. Remove paper backing. Referring to photo, follow **Almost Invisible Appliqué**, page 149, to appliqué motifs to wall hanging top.

COMPLETING THE WALL HANGING

1. Follow **Quilting**, page 151, **Quilting Diagram**, and **Flower Quilting Pattern** to mark, layer, and quilt.
2. Follow **Making a Hanging Sleeve**, page 157, to attach hanging sleeve to wall hanging.
3. Cut an 18" square of binding fabric. Follow **Making Continuous Bias Strip Binding**, page 155, to make approximately 3¹/₄ yds of 2¹/₂"w bias binding.
4. Follow **Attaching Binding with Mitered Corners**, page 155, to attach binding to wall hanging.

Wall Hanging Top Diagram

RUFFLED PATCHWORK PILLOW

SIZE: 15" x 15" (without ruffle)

YARDAGE REQUIREMENTS:

Yardage is based on 45"w fabric.

    25 fabric squares $3^1/2$" x $3^1/2$" (our pillow uses scraps from the **Spring Basket Wall Hanging**, page 65)

    $5/8$ yd for ruffle

    $15^1/2$" x $15^1/2$" square for backing

You will also need:

    polyester fiberfill

MAKING THE PILLOW

*Follow **Piecing and Pressing**, page 146, to make pillow top.*

1. Referring to photo, assemble 5 **squares** to make Row. Make 5 Rows. Assemble **Rows** to make **pillow top**.
2. Follow **Pillow Finishing**, page 157, to complete pillow with a 3" ruffle.

Quilting Diagram

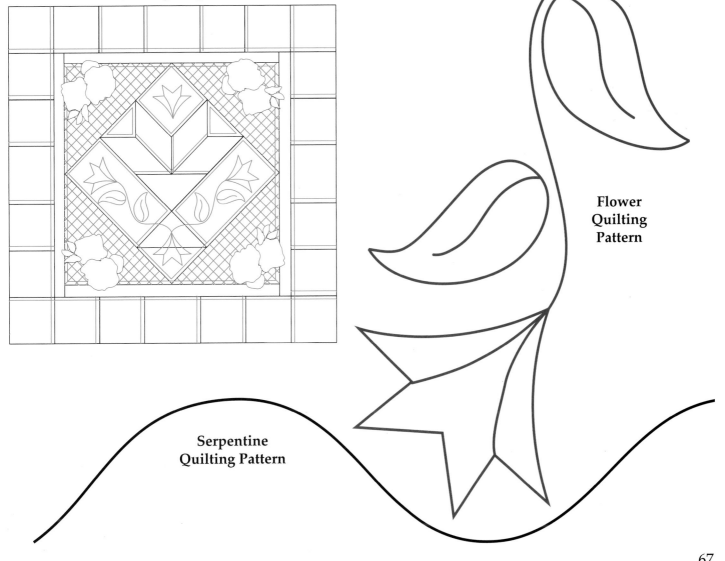

Flower Quilting Pattern

Serpentine Quilting Pattern

BOLD
COLLECTION

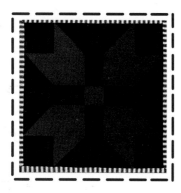

Vivid red and black fabrics lend
a bold look to a traditional pattern in
our Butterfly at the Crossroads quilt.
The bright "wings" seem to flutter to
life when contrasted against the dark
background. And working with only
two fabrics makes this simple pattern
even easier! You'll find it a breeze to
create a similar quilt by rotary cutting
all the basic squares and rectangles and
using our no-mistake grid method to make
the triangle pieces. With carefree diagonal
quilting, you'll net a fun-to-finish beauty!

Our Butterfly at the Crossroads pattern makes a fun-loving jump to den decor with these eye-catching accessories. So easy to sew, the oversized floor pillows feature the quilt block in reversed color schemes for a contrasting look. Just add borders in bright ticking stripes and prints and finish the cozy cushions with simple outline quilting. When the game's over, don't put away that coordinating checkerboard — it doubles as a wall hanging that will be the crowning accent for your room!

BUTTERFLY AT THE CROSSROADS QUILT

SKILL LEVEL: 1 2 3 4 5
BLOCK SIZE: 11½" x 11½"
QUILT SIZE: 66" x 76"

YARDAGE REQUIREMENTS
Yardage is based on 45"w fabric.

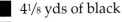

■ 4⅛ yds of black

■ 3⅛ yds of red
4¼ yds for backing
1 yd for binding
72" x 90" batting

CUTTING OUT THE PIECES
*All measurements include a ¼" seam allowance. Follow
Rotary Cutting, page 144, to cut fabric.*

1. **From black:** ■
   - Cut 6 selvage-to-selvage strips 2½"w. From these strips, cut a total of 16 **sashing strips** 2½" x 12".
   - Cut 12 selvage-to-selvage strips 2"w. From these strips, cut a total of 80 **rectangles** 2" x 5½".
   - Cut 6 selvage-to-selvage strips 3"w. From these strips, cut a total of 80 **squares** 3" x 3".
   - Cut 4 lengthwise strips 2" x 69" for **top/bottom borders**.
   - Cut 4 lengthwise strips 2" x 78" for **side borders**.
   - Cut 4 **large rectangles** 18" x 22" from remaining fabric width for triangle-squares.

2. **From red:** ■
   - Cut 1 selvage-to-selvage strip 2"w. From this strip, cut a total of 20 **center squares** 2" x 2".
   - Cut 6 selvage-to-selvage strips 3"w. From these strips, cut a total of 80 **squares** 3" x 3".
   - Cut 2 lengthwise strips 2" x 69" for **top/bottom borders**.
   - Cut 2 lengthwise strips 2" x 78" for **side borders**.
   - Cut 5 lengthwise strips 2½" x 66" for **sashing strips**.
   - Cut 4 **large rectangles** 18" x 22" from remaining fabric width for triangle-squares.

ASSEMBLING THE QUILT TOP
*Follow Piecing and Pressing, page 146, to make
quilt top.*

1. To make triangle-squares, place 1 red and 1 black **large rectangle** right sides together. Referring to **Fig. 1**, follow Steps 1 - 3 of **Making Triangle-Squares**, page 146, to mark a grid of 20 squares 3⅜" x 3⅜". Referring to **Fig. 2** for stitching directions, follow Steps 4 - 6 of **Making Triangle-Squares**, page 146, to complete 40 **triangle-squares**. Repeat with remaining **large rectangles** to make a total of 160 **triangle-squares**.

Fig. 1

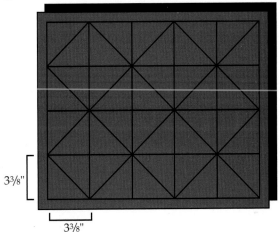

Fig. 2

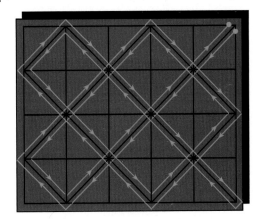

triangle-square (make 160)

2. Assemble 1 **square** and 1 **triangle-square** as shown to make **Unit 1**. Make 80 **Unit 1's**.

Unit 1 (make 80)

3. Assemble 1 **triangle-square** and 1 **square** as shown to make **Unit 2**. Make 80 **Unit 2's**.

Unit 2 (make 80)

4. Assemble 1 **Unit 1** and 1 **Unit 2** as shown to make **Unit 3**. Make 80 **Unit 3's**.

Unit 3 (make 80)

5. Assemble 2 **Unit 3's** and 1 **rectangle** as shown to make **Unit 4**. Make 40 **Unit 4's**.

Unit 4 (make 40)

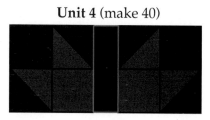

6. Assemble 2 **rectangles** and 1 **center square** as shown to make **Unit 5**. Make 20 **Unit 5's**.

Unit 5 (make 20)

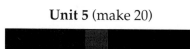

7. Assemble 2 **Unit 4's** and 1 **Unit 5** as shown to make **Block**. Make 20 **Blocks**.

Block (make 20)

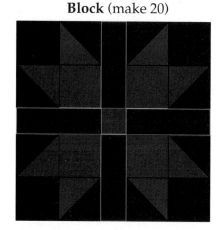

8. Assemble 5 **Blocks** and 4 **sashing strips** as shown to make **Row**. Make 4 **Rows**.

Row (make 4)

9. Referring to **Quilt Top Diagram**, assemble **Rows** and **sashing strips** to complete center section of quilt top.
10. Assemble borders as shown to make **Border Units**. Make 2 **Top/Bottom Border Units** and 2 **Side Border Units**.

Border Unit

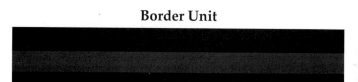

11. Follow **Adding Mitered Borders**, page 150, to attach **Border Units** to center section of quilt top to complete **Quilt Top**.

COMPLETING THE QUILT

1. Follow **Quilting**, page 151, and **Quilting Diagram** to mark, layer, and quilt.
2. Cut a 36" square of binding fabric. Follow **Making Continuous Bias Strip Binding**, page 155, to make approximately 8½ yds of 2½"w bias binding.
3. Follow **Attaching Binding with Mitered Corners**, page 155, to attach binding to quilt.

Quilt Top Diagram

Quilting Diagram

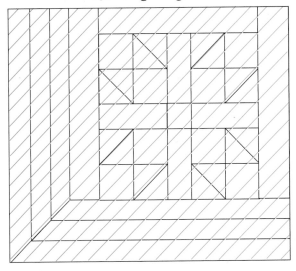

---- — QUICK TIP ---

THRIFTY QUILT BACKINGS

Sometimes a quilt top will be just a bit too wide to use 2 lengths of 45"w fabric for the backing. Instead of buying another full length of fabric, you might want to try piecing a section of the backing using leftover fabrics from your quilt top. For inspiration, see our Chinese Coins Quilt, shown on page 51. It features an expanded version of the strip-piecing technique described below.

1. *Determine how much extra width you will need to fit your quilt top. Two lengths of 45"w fabric, after shrinkage and trimming the selvages, will be approximately 82"w when sewn together. If your quilt top is 80"w, your backing will need to measure at least 88"w (see **Preparing Backing and Batting**, page 153), so you will need to add a 6"w section to your quilt backing.*
2. *Cut leftover fabrics from your quilt top into selvage-to-selvage strips that vary from 1"w to 3"w.*
3. *Sew the strips together in random color order to form a strip set.*
4. *From the strip set, cut sections the width you need to add to your quilt backing, plus seam allowances.*
5. *Sew these sections together until they measure the length of your quilt backing. Leftover strips from your quilt top that are shorter than selvage-to-selvage width may be trimmed and added to the pieced section, if necessary.*
6. *Sew the new pieced section and your backing pieces together. The pieced section may be added in the center between the 2 lengths of backing fabric or along 1 edge. You may even wish to set this piece off-center by cutting 1 length of backing fabric lengthwise and sewing the pieced section between the 2 pieces.*

FLOOR PILLOWS

PILLOW SIZE: 23" x 23"

Our coordinating floor pillows feature reversed colors in the center block. Follow Pillow A instructions to make a pillow with a small red center square or Pillow B instructions to make a pillow with a small black center square.

YARDAGE REQUIREMENTS
Yardage given is to make 1 Pillow A or 1 Pillow B and is based on 45"w fabric.

- ½ yd of black
- ½ yd of red
- ¼ yd of red print
- ½ yd of black and white stripe
- ½ yd for welting
- ¾ yd for pillow top backing
- ¾ yd for pillow back
- 3 yds of ½" cord for welting
- 26" x 26" batting
- polyester fiberfill

CUTTING OUT THE PIECES FOR PILLOW A OR PILLOW B
All measurements include a ¼" seam allowance. Follow Rotary Cutting, page 144, to cut fabric.

1. **From black:**

For Pillow A:

- Cut 1 **large square** 8" x 8" for triangle-squares.
- Cut 1 selvage-to-selvage strip 2"w. From this strip, cut 4 **rectangles** 2" x 5½".
- Cut 4 **squares** 3" x 3".
- Cut 4 **sashing squares** 2½" x 2½".

For Pillow B:

- Cut 1 **large square** 8" x 8" for triangle-squares.
- Cut 4 **squares** 3" x 3".
- Cut 1 **center square** 2" x 2".
- Cut 4 **sashing squares** 2½" x 2½".

2. **From red:**

For Pillow A:

- Cut 1 **large square** 8" x 8" for triangle-squares.
- Cut 4 **squares** 3" x 3".
- Cut 1 **center square** 2" x 2".

For Pillow B:

- Cut 1 **large square** 8" x 8" for triangle-squares.
- Cut 1 selvage-to-selvage strip 2"w. From this strip, cut 4 **rectangles** 2" x 5½".
- Cut 4 **squares** 3" x 3".

3. **From red print:**

For Pillow A or B:

- Cut 2 selvage-to-selvage strips 2½"w. From these strips, cut a total of 4 **sashing strips** 2½" x 15".

4. **From stripe:**

For Pillow A or B:

- Cut 2 selvage-to-selvage strips 2"w. From these strips, cut 4 **inner borders** 2" x 17½".
- Cut 4 selvage-to-selvage strips 2¾"w. From these strips, cut 4 **outer borders** 2¾" x 25½".

ASSEMBLING PILLOW TOP A
Follow Piecing and Pressing, page 146, to make pillow top.

1. To make triangle-squares, place red and black **large squares** right sides together. Referring to **Fig. 1**, follow Steps 1 - 3 of **Making Triangle-Squares**, page 146, to mark a grid of 4 squares 3⅜" x 3⅜". Referring to **Fig. 2** for stitching directions, follow Steps 4 - 6 of **Making Triangle-Squares**, page 146, to complete a total of 8 **triangle-squares**.

Fig. 1

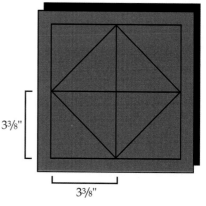

3⅜"

3⅜"

Fig. 2

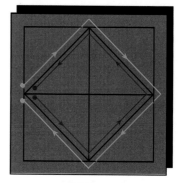

triangle-square (make 8)

2. Follow Steps 2 - 7 of **Assembling the Quilt Top** for **Butterfly at the Crossroads Quilt**, page 71, to make 1 **Block A** as shown.

Block A (make 1)

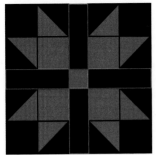

3. Follow **Adding Mitered Borders**, page 150, to attach **inner borders** to **Block A**.
4. Assemble 2 **sashing squares** and 1 **sashing strip** as shown to make **Unit 6**. Make 2 **Unit 6's**.

Unit 6 (make 2)

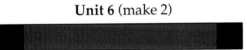

5. Referring to **Pillow Top A Diagram**, sew **sashing strips** and **Unit 6's** to **Block A**.
6. Follow **Adding Mitered Borders**, page 150, to attach **outer borders** to complete **Pillow Top A**.

ASSEMBLING PILLOW TOP B
1. Reversing the colors, follow Steps 1 and 2 of **Assembling Pillow Top A** to make **Block B** as shown.

Block B (make 1)

2. Follow Steps 3 - 6 of **Assembling Pillow Top A** to complete **Pillow Top B**.

COMPLETING PILLOW A *OR* PILLOW B
1. Follow **Quilting**, page 151, and **Quilting Diagram** to mark, layer, and quilt.
2. Follow **Pillow Finishing**, page 157, to complete pillow with welting.

Pillow Top A Diagram

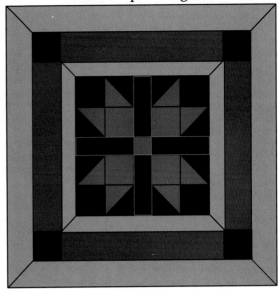

Quilting Diagram

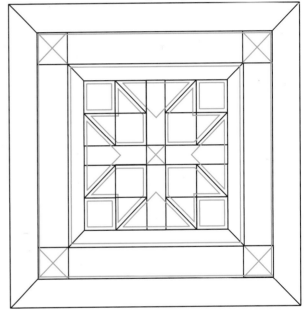

CHECKERBOARD WALL HANGING

SKILL LEVEL: 1 2 3 4 5
WALL HANGING SIZE: 19" x 30"

YARDAGE REQUIREMENTS
Yardage is based on 45"w fabric.

- ■ ½ yd of black
- ■ ¼ yd of red
- ■ ¼ yd of red print
- ■ ¼ yd of black and white stripe
  1 yd for backing and hanging sleeve
  23" x 34" batting

CUTTING OUT THE PIECES

All measurements include a ¹/₄" seam allowance. Follow
***Rotary Cutting**, page 144, to cut fabric.*

1. **From black:**
   - Cut 4 selvage-to-selvage **strips** 2¹/₂"w.
   - Cut 3 selvage-to-selvage strips 1³/₄"w. From these strips, cut 2 pieces 28¹/₂"l for **top/bottom borders** and 2 pieces 17¹/₂"l for **side borders**.
   - Cut 1 selvage-to-selvage **strip** 1¹/₂"w.

2. **From red:**
   - Cut 2 selvage-to-selvage **strips** 2¹/₂"w.

3. **From red print:**
   - Cut 2 selvage-to-selvage **strips** 2¹/₂"w.
   - Cut 1 selvage-to-selvage **strip** 1¹/₂"w.
   - Cut 4 **squares** 1³/₄" x 1³/₄".

4. **From stripe:**
   - Cut 4 selvage-to-selvage strips 1"w. From these strips, cut 4 **pieces** 16¹/₂"l. From remaining strips, cut 2 **pieces** 28¹/₂"l.

ASSEMBLING THE WALL HANGING TOP

*Follow **Piecing and Pressing**, page 146, to make wall hanging top.*

1. Assemble 2¹/₂"w **strips** as shown to make **Strip Set A**. Cut **Strip Set A** in half.

Strip Set A

2. Sew **Strip Set A** pieces together as shown to make **Strip Set B**. Cut across **Strip Set B** at 2¹/₂" intervals to make a total of 8 **Unit 1's**.

Strip Set B (make 1)   **Unit 1** (make 8)

2¹/₂"

3. Assemble **Unit 1's** as shown to make **Checkerboard Block**.

Checkerboard Block (make 1)

4. Assemble 2¹/₂"w and 1¹/₂"w **strips** as shown to make **Strip Set C**. Cut across **Strip Set C** at 2¹/₂" intervals to make a total of 8 **Unit 2's**.

Strip Set C (make 1)   **Unit 2** (make 8)

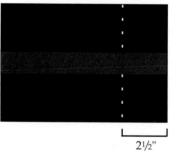

2¹/₂"

5. Assemble 2¹/₂"w and 1¹/₂"w **strips** as shown to make **Strip Set D**. Cut across **Strip Set D** at 1¹/₂" intervals to make a total of 4 **Unit 3's**. Cut across remainder of **Strip Set D** at 6¹/₂" intervals to make a total of 2 **Unit 4's**.

Strip Set D (make 1)   **Unit 3** (make 4)   **Unit 4** (make 2)

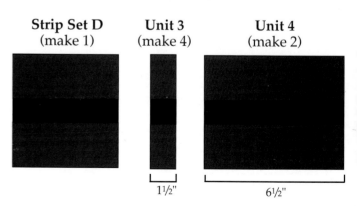

1¹/₂"   6¹/₂"

6. Assemble 2 **Unit 2's** and 1 **Unit 3** as shown to make **Unit 5**. Make 4 **Unit 5's**.

Unit 5 (make 4)

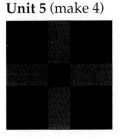

7. Assemble 2 **Unit 5's** and 1 **Unit 4** as shown to make **Unit 6**. Make 2 **Unit 6's**.

Unit 6 (make 2)

8. Assemble $16^{1}/{2}$"l **pieces**, **Unit 6's**, and **Checkerboard Block** as shown to make 1 **Unit 7**.

Unit 7 (make 1)

9. Referring to **Wall Hanging Top Diagram**, sew $28^{1}/{2}$"l **pieces** to top and bottom of **Unit 7** to complete center section of wall hanging top.

10. Assemble 2 **squares** and **top/bottom border** as shown to make **Border Unit**. Make 2 **Border Units**.

Border Unit (make 2)

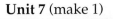

11. Referring to **Wall Hanging Top Diagram**, sew **side borders**, then **Border Units** to center section of wall hanging top to complete **Wall Hanging Top**.

COMPLETING THE WALL HANGING

1. Cut backing and batting same size as wall hanging top.
2. Place backing and wall hanging top right sides together. Place batting on wrong side of wall hanging top. Leaving a 6" opening for turning, use a $^{1}/{2}$" seam allowance to sew top, backing, and batting together. Cut corners diagonally, trim batting close to seamline, turn right side out, and press. Blindstitch opening closed.
3. Follow **Marking Quilting Lines**, page 151, and **Quilting Diagram** to mark wall hanging. Refer to **The Quilting Stitch**, page 153, to quilt along marked lines and in the ditch along indicated seamlines.
4. To make hanging sleeve, cut one 3" x 29" strip from backing fabric. Press all edges $^{1}/{4}$" to wrong side; press $^{1}/{4}$" to wrong side again. Sew along pressed edges.
5. With 1 long edge of hanging sleeve just below top of wall hanging, center and pin hanging sleeve to backing. Blindstitch long edges of hanging sleeve to backing.

Wall Hanging Top Diagram

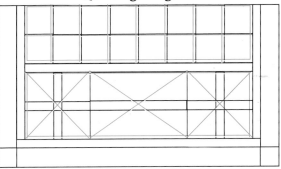

Quilting Diagram

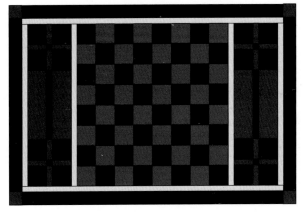

77

WILD GOOSE CHASE

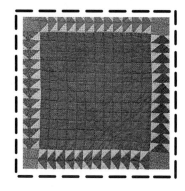

Resembling the striking formations of migrating flocks, the Wild Goose Chase is an easy-to-sew pattern that's beloved for its dramatic style. The antique beauty shown here inspired us to create a similar quilt — but we've simplified the work by calling for fewer fabrics for the triangles. The quilt is made even easier by using a quicker method for creating the triangle sashing strips and then setting them off with large single blocks. Faster and more accurate than the traditional way, these techniques will help you create a charming quilt that you'll treasure.

WILD GOOSE CHASE QUILT

SKILL LEVEL: 1 2 3 4 5
BLOCK SIZE: 12" x 12"
QUILT SIZE: 79" x 89"

YARDAGE REQUIREMENTS

Yardage is based on 45"w fabric.

- 5 yds of brown print
- 2 yds **total** of assorted brown prints
- 2½ yds **total** of assorted off-white prints
- ⅜ yd of pink print
- 2½ yds of off-white print for inner borders (**or** ⅝ yd for pieced borders)
- 1 yd of brown stripe for binding
- 6 yds for backing
- 90" x 108" batting

CUTTING OUT THE PIECES

All measurements include a ¹/₄" seam allowance. Follow
Rotary Cutting*, page 144, to cut fabric.*

1. **From brown print:**

   - Cut 2 lengthwise strips 3" x 93" for **side outer borders**.
   - Cut 2 lengthwise strips 3" x 85" for **top/bottom outer borders.**
   - Cut 10 strips 12½"w x remaining fabric width. From these strips, cut a total of 21 **setting squares** 12½" x 12½".

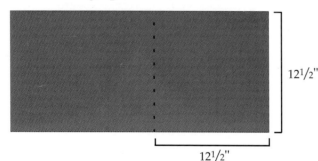

setting square (cut 21)

- Cut 4 squares 18¼" x 18¼". Cut each square twice diagonally to make 16 **side setting triangles** (you will need 13 and have 3 left over).

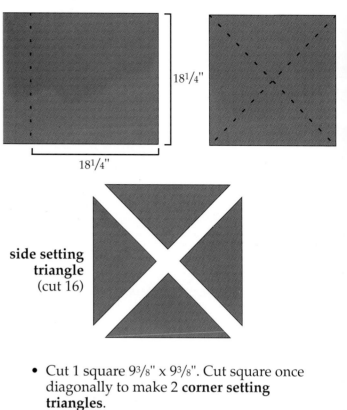

side setting triangle (cut 16)

- Cut 1 square 9⅜" x 9⅜". Cut square once diagonally to make 2 **corner setting triangles**.

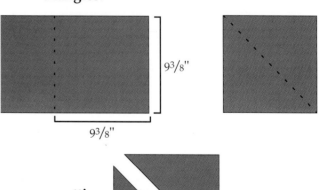

corner setting triangle (cut 2)

2. **From assorted brown prints:**

   - Cut a total of 24 selvage-to-selvage strips 2½"w. From these strips, cut 672 **rectangles** 1½" x 2½".

rectangle (cut 672)

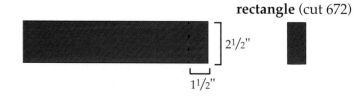

80

3. From assorted off-white prints:
- Cut a total of 48 selvage-to-selvage strips 1½"w. From these strips, cut 1,344 **squares** 1½" x 1½".

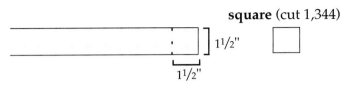

square (cut 1,344)

4. From pink print: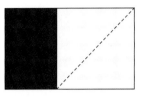
- Cut 2 selvage-to-selvage strips 2½"w. From these strips, cut a total of 21 **sashing squares** 2½" x 2½".

sashing square (cut 21)

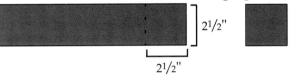

- Cut 4 squares 4⅛" x 4⅛". Cut each square twice diagonally to make 16 **side sashing triangles** (you will need 13 and have 3 left over).

side sashing triangle (cut 16)

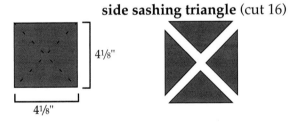

- Cut 1 square 2¼" x 2¼". Cut square once diagonally to make 2 **corner sashing triangles**.

corner sashing triangle (cut 2)

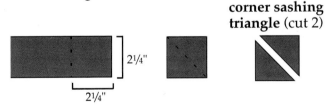

5. From off-white print for inner border:

(2½ yds)
- Cut 2 lengthwise strips 2" x 74" for **top/bottom inner borders**.
- Cut 2 lengthwise strips 2" x 87" for **side inner borders**.

OR

(⅝ yd)
- Cut 8 selvage-to-selvage strips 2"w. Piece and trim strips to make 2 pieces 2" x 74" for **top/bottom inner borders** and 2 pieces 2" x 87" for **side inner borders**.

ASSEMBLING THE QUILT TOP

*Follow **Piecing and Pressing**, page 146, to make quilt top.*

1. Place 1 **square** on 1 **rectangle** and stitch diagonally as shown in **Fig. 1**. Trim ¼" from stitching line as shown in **Fig. 2**. Press open, pressing seam allowance toward brown fabric.

Fig. 1

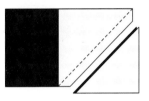

Fig. 2

2. Place a matching **square** on opposite end of **rectangle**. Stitch diagonally as shown in **Fig. 3**. Trim ¼" from stitching line as shown in **Fig. 4**. Press open, pressing seam allowance toward brown fabric (**Fig. 5**).

Fig. 3

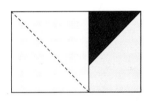

Fig. 4

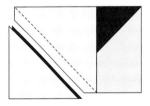

Fig. 5

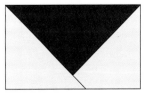

3. Repeat Steps 1 and 2 to make a total of 672 **Unit 1's**.

Unit 1 (make 672)

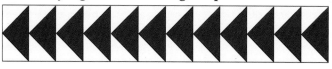

4. Assemble 12 **Unit 1's** to make **Flying Geese Sashing Strip**. Make 56 **Flying Geese Sashing Strips.**

Flying Geese Sashing Strip (make 56)

Assembly Diagram

5. Follow **Assembly Diagram** to assemble **setting squares**, **side** and **corner setting triangles**, **Flying Geese Sashing Strips**, **sashing squares**, and **side** and **corner sashing triangles** into rows; sew rows together to complete center section of quilt top.
6. Follow **Adding Squared Borders**, page 150, and **Quilt Top Diagram** to add **top**, **bottom**, and then **side inner borders**. Add **top**, **bottom** and then **side outer borders** to complete **Quilt Top**.

COMPLETING THE QUILT

1. Follow **Quilting**, page 151, and **Quilting Diagram** to mark, layer, and quilt.
2. Cut a 36" square of binding fabric. Follow **Making Continuous Bias Strip Binding**, page 155, to make approximately 10 yds of 2¹/₂"w bias binding.
3. Follow **Attaching Binding with Mitered Corners**, page 155, to attach binding to quilt.

Quilting Diagram

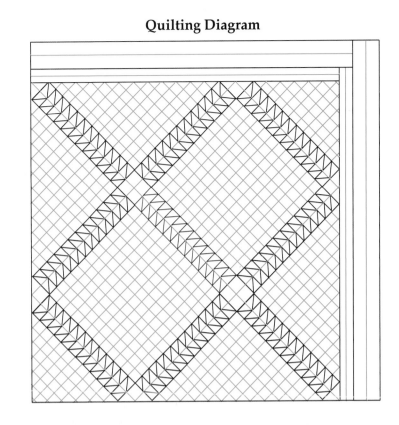

Quilt Top Diagram

CRIB QUILTS

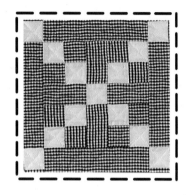

The simple charm of the Irish Chain pattern continues to enchant quilters of today, just as it did during Colonial times. Quilts fashioned in such cherished designs were often crafted to mark special events, especially the birth of a baby. In that thoughtful tradition, we were inspired by the feminine antique crib quilt on page 86 to create this masculine version for boys. A dramatic change took place when we reversed the colored and white areas and added a bright border of train appliqués. To save time, the fabrics for the quilt top were rotary cut and then pieced using easy-to-assemble strips and large single blocks. And the border motifs were machine appliquéd with clear thread, so you won't have to stop and change thread colors. Complemented by crosshatch quilting, this cover-up will keep a little boy right on track for naptime!

Your baby girl will be pretty in pink when you re-create this precious antique crib quilt for her. It's child's play to sew by rotary cutting the fabrics and then piecing them in strip sets and large single blocks. The pink-on-white color scheme for this Irish Chain pattern provides a soft look, and a sweet Ice-Cream Cone border creates a delicate scalloped edging. Diamond-look crosshatch quilting will make this quilt a girl's best friend!

STRAWBERRY SUNDAE CRIB QUILT

SKILL LEVEL: 1 2 **3** 4 5
BLOCK SIZE: 6¼" x 6¼"
QUILT SIZE: 38" x 51"

YARDAGE REQUIREMENTS
Yardage is based on 45"w fabric.

☐ 2 yds of white
◼ 1 yd of pink
　1⅝ yds for backing
　¾ yd for binding
　45" x 60" batting

CUTTING OUT THE PIECES
*All measurements include a ¼" seam allowance. To make templates from patterns **A**, **B**, and **C**, page 91, use a permanent fine-point marker to trace patterns onto template plastic. Label and cut out templates. Follow **Rotary Cutting**, page 144, to cut other pieces.*

1. **From white:** ☐
   - Cut 6 selvage-to-selvage **strips** 1¾"w.
   - Cut 2 selvage-to-selvage **strips** 3"w.
   - Cut 2 selvage-to-selvage **strips** 3"w. From these strips, cut a total of 36 **rectangles** 1¾" x 3".
   - Cut 3 selvage-to-selvage strips 6¾"w. From these strips, cut a total of 17 **squares** 6¾" x 6¾".
   - Cut 48 **B's** using Template B.
   - Cut 4 **C's** using Template C.

2. **From pink:** ◼
   - Cut 7 selvage-to-selvage **strips** 1¾"w.
   - Cut 44 **A's** using Template A.
   - Cut 8 **C's** using Template C.

ASSEMBLING THE QUILT TOP
*Follow **Piecing and Pressing**, page 146, to make quilt top.*

1. Assemble 1¾"w **strips** as shown to make **Strip Set A**. Make 6 **Strip Set A's**. Cut across **Strip Set A's** at 1¾" intervals to make a total of 144 **Unit 1's**.

Strip Set A (make 6)　　**Unit 1** (make 144)

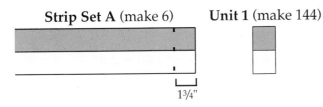

1¾"

2. Assemble 2 **Unit 1's** as shown to make **Unit 2**. Make 72 **Unit 2's**.

Unit 2 (make 72)

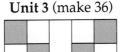

3. Assemble 2 **Unit 2's** and 1 **rectangle** as shown to make **Unit 3**. Make 36 **Unit 3's**.

Unit 3 (make 36)

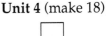

4. Assemble **strips** as shown to make **Strip Set B**. Cut across **Strip Set B** at 1¾" intervals to make a total of 18 **Unit 4's**.

Strip Set B (make 1)　　**Unit 4** (make 18)

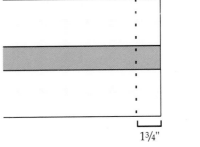

1¾"

5. Assemble 2 **Unit 3's** and 1 **Unit 4** as shown to make **Block**. Make 18 **Blocks**.

Block (make 18)

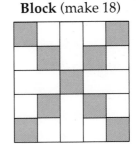

6. Referring to **Quilt Top Diagram**, page 88, assemble **Blocks** and **squares** into rows; sew rows together to complete center section of quilt top.

7. For each **Top/Bottom Border**, assemble 9 **A's**, 10 **B's**, and 2 **C's** as shown. For each **Side Border**, assemble 13 **A's**, 14 **B's**, and 2 **C's** as shown. Referring to **Quilt Top Diagram**, attach **Borders** to center section of quilt top.

Top/Bottom Border (make 2)

Side Border (make 2)

8. Follow Steps 2 and 3 of **Working with Diamond Shapes**, page 147, to sew 1 white **C** into each corner of border to complete **Quilt Top**.

COMPLETING THE QUILT

1. Follow **Quilting**, page 151, and **Quilting Diagram** to mark, layer, and quilt.
2. Cut a 22" square of binding fabric. Follow **Making Continuous Bias Strip Binding**, page 155, to make approximately 5¹/₂ yds of 1¹/₂"w bias binding.
3. Follow Steps 1 and 2 of **Attaching Binding with Mitered Corners**, page 155, and pin binding to front of quilt. Sew binding to quilt, leaving a 2" overlap. Trim off excess binding and stitch overlap in place. Fold binding over to quilt backing and pin in place, covering stitching line. Blindstitch binding to backing.

Quilt Top Diagram

Quilting Diagram

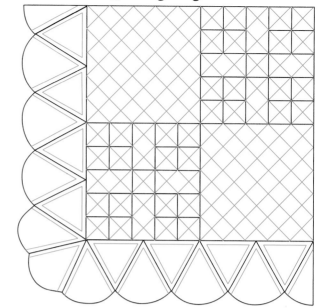

CHOO-CHOO CRIB QUILT

SKILL LEVEL: 1 2 3 4 5
BLOCK SIZE: 6¹/₄" x 6¹/₄"
QUILT SIZE: 42" x 55"

YARDAGE REQUIREMENTS

Yardage is based on 45"w fabric.

▨ 2¹/₄ yds of blue check

☐ ¹/₂ yd of white

◪ scraps of primary colors for train appliqué
2⁷/₈ yds for backing
³/₄ yd for binding
45" x 60" batting

You will also need:
paper-backed fusible web
transparent monofilament thread for appliqué

CUTTING OUT THE PIECES

All measurements include a ¹/₄" seam allowance. Follow Rotary Cutting, page 144, to cut fabric.

1. **From blue check:** ▨
   - Cut 2 lengthwise strips 5¹/₂" x 46" for **side borders**.
   - Cut 2 lengthwise strips 5¹/₂" x 34" for **top/bottom borders**.
   - Cut 6 strips 6³/₄"w x remaining fabric width. From these strips, cut a total of 17 **squares** 6³/₄" x 6³/₄".
   - Cut 6 selvage-to-selvage **strips** 1³/₄"w.
   - Cut 2 selvage-to-selvage **strips** 3"w.
   - Cut 2 selvage-to-selvage **strips** 3"w. From these strips, cut a total of 36 **rectangles** 1³/₄" x 3".
   - Cut 1 strip 5¹/₂" x 22". From this strip, cut 4 **border squares** 5¹/₂" x 5¹/₂".

2. **From white:**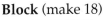
   - Cut 7 selvage-to-selvage **strips** 1¾"w.

3. **From scraps:**
   - Use patterns, pages 90 and 91, and follow **Preparing Appliqué Pieces**, page 148, to cut the following number of appliqué pieces :

A — 4	I — 6	Q — 8
B — 4	J — 6	R — 4
C — 4	K — 30	S — 4
D — 4	L — 6	T — 8
E — 4	M — 4	U — 8
F — 4	N — 4	V — 4
G — 4	O — 4	
H — 48	P — 8	

ASSEMBLING THE QUILT TOP

*Follow **Piecing and Pressing**, page 146, to make quilt top.*

1. Assemble 1¾"w strips as shown to make **Strip Set A**. Make 6 **Strip Set A's**. Cut across **Strip Set A's** at 1¾" intervals to make a total of 144 **Unit 1's**.

Strip Set A (make 6)   **Unit 1** (make 144)

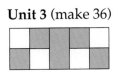

2. Assemble 2 **Unit 1's** as shown to make **Unit 2**. Make 72 **Unit 2's**.

Unit 2 (make 72)

3. Assemble 2 **Unit 2's** and 1 **rectangle** as shown to make **Unit 3**. Make 36 **Unit 3's**.

Unit 3 (make 36)

4. Assemble strips as shown to make **Strip Set B**. Cut across **Strip Set B** at 1¾" intervals to make a total of 18 **Unit 4's**.

Strip Set B (make 1)   **Unit 4** (make 18)

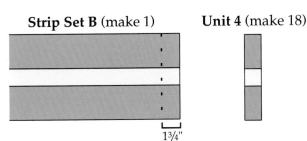

5. Assemble 2 **Unit 3's** and 1 **Unit 4** as shown to make **Block**. Make 18 **Blocks**.

Block (make 18)

6. Referring to **Quilt Top Diagram**, assemble **Blocks** and **squares** into rows; sew rows together to complete center section of quilt top.

7. For train border, follow **Almost Invisible Appliqué**, page 149, and **Quilt Top Diagram** to appliqué pieces to **top/bottom borders**, **side borders**, and **border squares**.

8. Attach 1 **border square** to each end of each **side border**. Referring to **Quilt Top Diagram**, attach **top**, **bottom**, and then **side borders** to center section of quilt top to complete **Quilt Top**.

COMPLETING THE QUILT

1. Follow **Quilting**, page 151, and **Quilting Diagram**, page 90, to mark, layer, and quilt.

2. Cut a 27" square of binding fabric. Follow **Making Continuous Bias Strip Binding**, page 155, to make approximately 6 yds of 2½"w bias binding.

3. Follow **Attaching Binding with Mitered Corners**, page 155, to attach binding to quilt.

Quilt Top Diagram

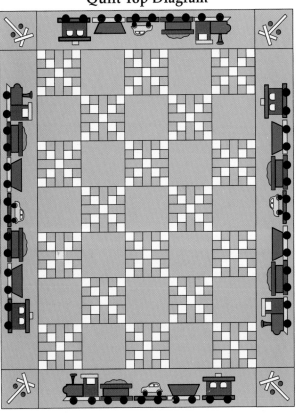

Quilting Diagram

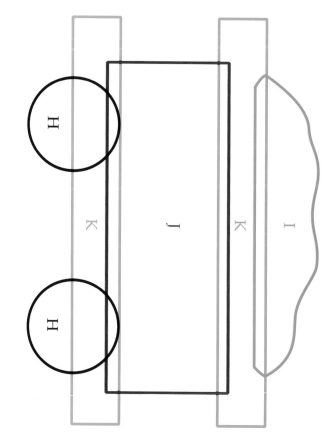

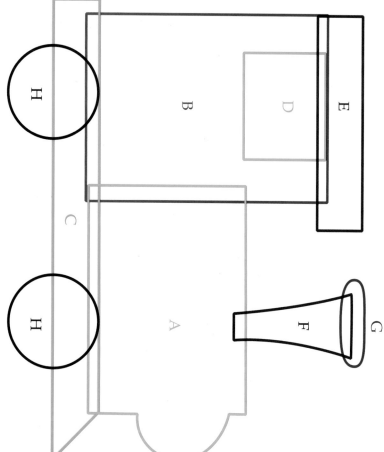

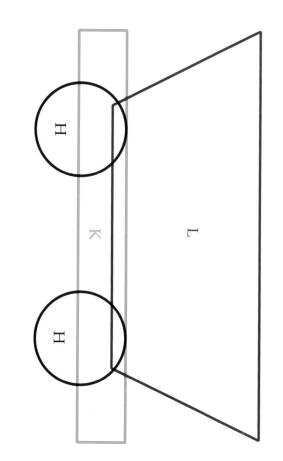

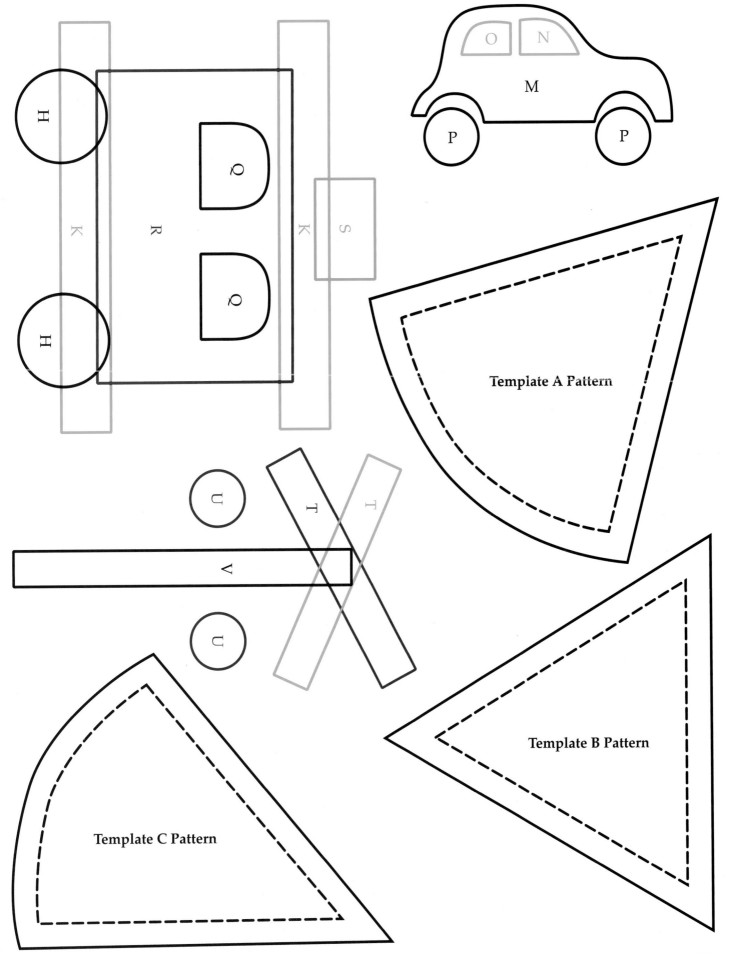

Template A Pattern

Template B Pattern

Template C Pattern

SCOTTIE COLLECTION

During the 1930's, Americans fell in love with a little Scottish terrier named Fala, whose perkiness and cute antics garnered almost as much publicity as his owner — President Franklin Roosevelt. Naturally, quilters incorporated the popular pet into their designs, and mail-order magazines offered several Scottie patterns for sale. To capture that nostalgic charm, we created a whole collection of Scottie-inspired piecework. Complementing the set, colorful plaids and stripes combine for a handsome spread that's even easy for beginners to assemble. And finishing the quilt couldn't be faster — just use embroidery floss and buttons to tie the layers into a plush comforter!

You'll see results in no time when you quilt our adorable pillow (below) and wall hanging (opposite). As the foundation for both projects, the Scottie quilt block is easily rotary cut, and our quick grid technique speeds piecing. Simply finish the block as a pillow and add a cute ruffle, or piece several Scottie blocks and offset them with plaid bow-tie blocks to create a decorative room accent. Fast in-the-ditch quilting completes the pillow, with stitched diagonals and zigzags adding interest to the wall hanging.

This playful jumper is perfect for a walk in the park with your favorite pooch! We simply sewed a cute appliquéd Scottie block pocket onto a ready-made dress and then added matching trims to create the fun outfit.

PLAID QUILT

SKILL LEVEL: 1 2 3 4 5
BLOCK SIZE: 16¹/₂" x 16¹/₂"
QUILT SIZE: 84" x 100"

YARDAGE REQUIREMENTS
Yardage is based on 45"w fabric.

 4¹/₄ yds **total** of dark plaids (our quilt uses 11 different dark plaids)

3¹/₂ yds **total** of light plaids and stripes (our quilt uses 9 different light plaids and stripes)
8¹/₂ yds for backing
1 yd for binding
90" x 108" batting

You will also need:
black embroidery floss
20 black 1" buttons

CUTTING OUT THE PIECES
All measurements include a ¹/₄" seam allowance. Follow **Rotary Cutting***, page 144, to cut fabric.*

1. **From dark plaids:**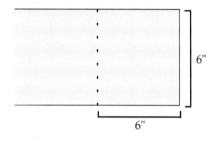
   - Cut a **total** of 46 selvage-to-selvage **strips** 3¹/₄"w.

2. **From light plaids and stripes:** ☐
   - Cut a **total** of 20 selvage-to-selvage strips 6"w. From these strips, cut a total of 135 **squares** 6" x 6".

square (cut 135)

6"

6"

ASSEMBLING THE QUILT TOP
Follow **Piecing and Pressing***, page 146, to make quilt top. To achieve the scrappy look of our quilt, assemble strips, squares, and units in random fabric combinations.*

1. Assemble **strips** as shown to make **Strip Set A**. Make 23 **Strip Set A's**. Cut across **Strip Set A's** at 3¹/₄" intervals to make **Unit 1**. Make a total of 270 **Unit 1's**.

Strip Set A (make 23)   **Unit 1** (make 270)

3¹/₄"

2. Assemble 2 **Unit 1's** as shown to make **Unit 2**. Make 135 **Unit 2's**.

Unit 2 (make 135)

3. Assemble 2 **squares** and 1 **Unit 2** as shown to make **Unit 3**. Make 45 **Unit 3's**. Assemble 2 **Unit 2's** and 1 **square** as shown to make **Unit 4**. Make 45 **Unit 4's**.

Unit 3 (make 45)

Unit 4 (make 45)

4. Assemble 2 **Unit 3's** and 1 **Unit 4** as shown to make **Block A**. Make 15 **Block A's**. Assemble 2 **Unit 4's** and 1 **Unit 3** as shown to make **Block B**. Make 15 **Block B's**.

Block A (make 15)   **Block B (make 15)**

5. Referring to **Quilt Top Diagram**, assemble **Blocks** into rows; sew rows together to complete **Quilt Top**.

COMPLETING THE QUILT

1. Follow **Quilting**, page 151, to layer and tie quilt. Tie quilt at outside corners of **Unit 2's**. Before trimming floss ends, refer to **Quilt Top Diagram** to attach buttons to corners of **Blocks**.

2. Cut a 36" square of binding fabric. Follow **Making Continuous Bias Strip Binding**, page 155, to make approximately 11 yds of 2¹/₂"w bias binding.

3. Follow **Attaching Binding with Overlapped Corners**, page 156, to attach binding to quilt.

Quilt Top Diagram

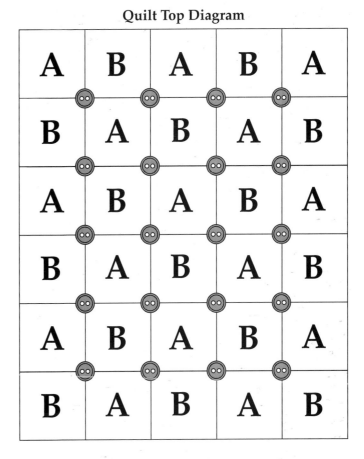

SCOTTIE WALL HANGING

SKILL LEVEL: 1 2 3 4 5
BLOCK SIZE: 9" x 9"
WALL HANGING SIZE: 34" x 34"

YARDAGE REQUIREMENTS
Yardage is based on 45"w fabric.

☐ ¹/₂ yd of white

■ ³/₈ yd of black

▥ ¹/₄ yd **each** of 2 different stripes

◪ scraps of assorted plaids (our wall hanging uses 13 different plaids)
  1¹/₈ yds for backing and hanging sleeve
  ¹/₂ yd for binding
  45" x 60" batting

You will also need:
  4 black 1" buttons
  5 red 1" buttons

CUTTING OUT THE PIECES

All measurements include a ¹/₄" seam allowance. Follow **Rotary Cutting**, *page 144, to cut fabric.*

1. **From white:**
   - Cut 2 selvage-to-selvage strips 2"w. From these strips, cut a total of 8 **small rectangles** 2" x 6¹/₂". From remainder of strips, cut a total of 12 **small squares** 2" x 2".
   - Cut 1 selvage-to-selvage strip 2"w. From this strip, cut a total of 4 **medium rectangles** 2" x 9¹/₂".
   - Cut 1 selvage-to-selvage strip 3¹/₂"w. From this strip, cut a total of 4 **medium squares** 3¹/₂" x 3¹/₂".
   - Cut 1 **large rectangle** 6" x 16" for triangle-squares.

2. **From black:** ■
   - Cut 1 selvage-to-selvage strip 2"w. From this strip, cut a total of 8 **small squares** 2" x 2". From remainder of strip, cut a total of 4 **small rectangles** 2" x 5".
   - Cut 1 **large rectangle** 6" x 16" for triangle-squares.

3. **From *each* stripe:** ▥
   - Cut 1 selvage-to-selvage strip 5"w from each fabric. From each strip, cut a total of 5 **large squares** 5" x 5".

4. **From assorted plaids:** ◪
   - Cut a total of 4 assorted **medium squares** 3¹/₂" x 3¹/₂" for dog coats.
   - Cut a total of 10 assorted **large squares** 5" x 5" for large pieces in Bow Tie Blocks.
   - Cut 1 selvage-to-selvage strip 2"w from 1 plaid. From this strip, cut a total of 10 **small squares** 2" x 2" for bow ties in Bow Tie Blocks.
   - Cut a total of 4 assorted rectangles 1³/₄" x 7" for **bows**.
   - Cut 3¹/₂"w assorted pieces that vary in length from 6¹/₂" to 16¹/₂" for **outer border pieces**.

ASSEMBLING THE WALL HANGING TOP

Follow **Piecing and Pressing**, *page 146, to make wall hanging top.*

SCOTTIE DOG BLOCKS

1. To make triangle-squares, place white and black **large rectangles** right sides together. Referring to **Fig. 1**, follow Steps 1 - 3 of **Making Triangle-Squares**, page 146, to draw a grid of 12 squares 2³/₈" x 2³/₈". Referring to **Fig. 2** for sewing directions, follow Steps 4 - 6 of **Making Triangle-Squares**, page 146, to make a total of 24 **triangle-squares**.

Fig. 1

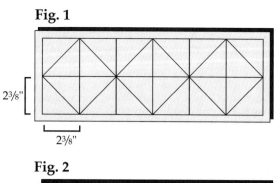

Fig. 2

triangle-square (make 24)

2. Assemble 1 **triangle-square** and 1 **small square** as shown to make **Unit 1**. Make 4 **Unit 1's**. Assemble 2 **triangle-squares** as shown to make **Unit 2**. Make 4 **Unit 2's**.

Unit 1 (make 4)   **Unit 2** (make 4)

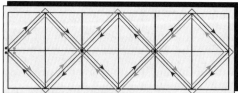

3. Assemble 1 **Unit 1**, 1 **Unit 2**, and 1 **medium square** as shown to make **Unit 3**. Make 4 **Unit 3's**.

Unit 3 (make 4)

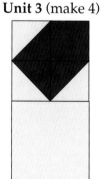

4. Assemble 1 **triangle-square** and 1 **small square** as shown to make **Unit 4**. Make 4 **Unit 4's**. Assemble 2 **small squares** as shown to make **Unit 5**. Make 4 **Unit 5's**.

Unit 4 (make 4)   **Unit 5** (make 4)

     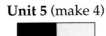

5. Assemble 1 **Unit 4**, 1 **medium square**, and 1 **Unit 5** as shown to make **Unit 6**. Make 4 **Unit 6's**.

Unit 6 (make 4)

6. Assemble 1 **triangle-square** and 1 **small rectangle** as shown to make **Unit 7**. Make 4 **Unit 7's**.

Unit 7 (make 4)

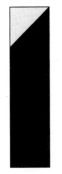

7. Assemble 1 **Unit 7** and 1 **small rectangle** as shown to make **Unit 8**. Make 4 **Unit 8's**.

Unit 8 (make 4)

8. Assemble 1 **Unit 3**, 1 **Unit 6**, and 1 **Unit 8** as shown to make **Unit 9**. Make 4 **Unit 9's**.

Unit 9 (make 4)

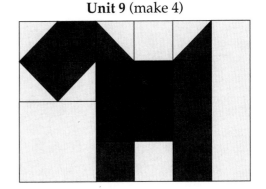

9. Assemble 1 **small square**, 1 **triangle-square**, and 1 **small rectangle** as shown to make **Unit 10**. Make 4 **Unit 10's**.

Unit 10 (make 4)

10. Assemble 1 **Unit 10**, 1 **Unit 9**, and 1 **medium rectangle** as shown to make **Scottie Dog Block**. Make 4 **Scottie Dog Blocks**.

Scottie Dog Block (make 4)

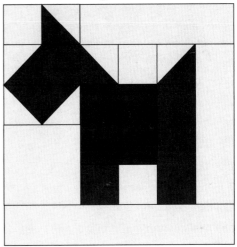

BOW TIE BLOCKS

1. Referring to **Wall Hanging Top Diagram** and photo, lay out **Scottie Dog Blocks** and large **squares** to determine final placement. Mark corners of squares where bow tie pieces will be placed (**Fig. 3**).

Fig. 3

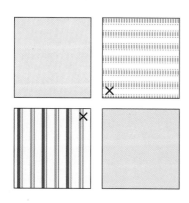

2. Place 1 plaid **small square** on marked corner of 1 **large square** and sew a diagonal line as shown in **Fig. 4**. Trim seam allowance to ¼" as shown in **Fig. 5** and press to make **Unit 11**. Make 10 **Unit 11's**.

Fig. 4	Fig. 5	Unit 11 (make 10)

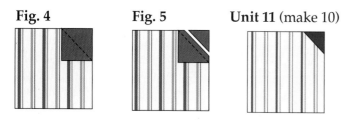

3. Assemble 2 **large squares** and 2 **Unit 11's** as shown to make 1 **Bow Tie Block**. Make 5 **Bow Tie Blocks**.

Bow Tie Block (make 5)

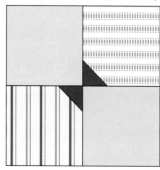

COMPLETING THE WALL HANGING TOP

1. Referring to **Wall Hanging Top Diagram**, assemble **Scottie Dog Blocks** and **Bow Tie Blocks** to complete center section of wall hanging top.
2. Sew **outer border pieces** together to make 1 **left border** 3½" x 27½", 1 **bottom border** 3½" x 30½", 1 **right border** 3½" x 30½", and 1 **top border** 3½" x 33½". Sew **left**, **bottom**, **right**, and then **top borders** to center section of wall hanging top to complete **Wall Hanging Top**.

COMPLETING THE WALL HANGING

1. Follow **Quilting**, page 151, and **Quilting Diagram** to mark, layer, and quilt.
2. Follow **Making A Hanging Sleeve**, page 157, to attach hanging sleeve to wall hanging.
3. Cut an 18" square of binding fabric. Follow **Making Continuous Bias Strip Binding**, page 155, to make approximately 4½ yds of 2½"w bias binding.
4. Follow **Attaching Binding with Overlapped Corners**, page 156, to attach binding to wall hanging.
5. For bow on each dog, fold 1 **bow** in half with right sides together and matching short edges. Leaving an opening for turning, sew raw edges together. Cut corners diagonally, turn right side out, and press. Blindstitch opening closed. Knot a length of thread securely around center to gather **bow**.
6. Referring to photo, sew **bows** and buttons to wall hanging.

Wall Hanging Top Diagram

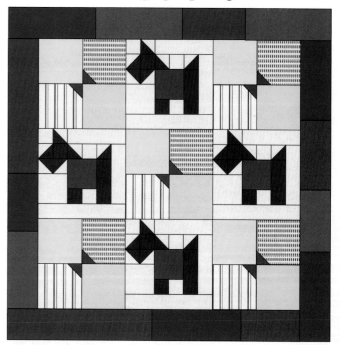

Quilting Diagram

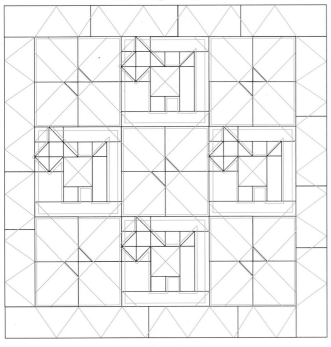

╭ ─ ─ ─ ─ ─ ─ ─ ─ ─ ─ ╮

QUICK TIP

USING PLAIDS AND STRIPES

Mixing lots of stripes and plaids in a single project is not as difficult as you might think when you keep the following guidelines in mind:

Think about plaids and stripes as you would any other print fabric.

- *Do your plaids and stripes fall into pleasing color families?*
- *Do you have a variety of scales in your fabrics? Are some plaids large-scale and some smaller scale? Is the same true for your striped fabrics?*
- *Will some of your fabrics "act like" background fabrics, while others may be bolder "feature fabrics"?*

Cutting plaids and stripes doesn't have to be an ordeal either.

- *If your plaids and stripes are woven, take care to align your cuts carefully with the grain of the fabric.*
- *If your fabrics are printed, consider aligning your cuts with the "visual grainline" — the straight lines of the design — even if the design doesn't match the true fabric grain.*
- *Or, you may ignore the "visual grainline" of printed fabrics altogether. Many of today's scrappy projects get their old-fashioned charm from plaids and stripes with designs that "veer off" the edges of the cut pieces.*

╰ ─ ─ ─ ─ ─ ─ ─ ─ ─ ─ ╯

SCOTTIE PILLOW

PILLOW SIZE: 14 x 14" (without ruffle)

YARDAGE REQUIREMENTS

Yardage is based on 45"w fabric.

- ☐ $3/8$ yd of white
- ■ $1/4$ yd of black
- ▥ $1/8$ yd of blue and white stripe
- ◩ scraps of assorted plaids (our pillow uses 9 different plaids)
  $1/2$ yd for pillow top backing
  $1\frac{1}{4}$ yds for pillow back and ruffle
  18" x 18" batting

You will also need:
  1 red 1" button
  polyester fiberfill

CUTTING OUT THE PIECES

All measurements include a $1/4$" seam allowance. Follow **Rotary Cutting**, *page 144, to cut fabric.*

1. **From white:** ☐
   - Cut 1 selvage-to-selvage strip 2"w. From this strip, cut 3 **small squares** 2" x 2", 2 **small rectangles** 2" x $6\frac{1}{2}$", and 1 **medium rectangle** 2" x $9\frac{1}{2}$".
   - Cut 1 **medium square** $3\frac{1}{2}$" x $3\frac{1}{2}$".
   - Cut 1 **large square** 6" x 6" for triangle-squares.

2. **From black:** ■
   - Cut 2 **small squares** 2" x 2".
   - Cut 1 **small rectangle** 2" x 5".
   - Cut 1 **large square** 6" x 6" for triangle-squares.

3. **From stripe:** ▥
   - Cut 1 selvage-to-selvage strip $1\frac{1}{2}$"w. From this strip, cut 2 pieces $1\frac{1}{2}$" x $9\frac{1}{2}$" for **top/bottom inner borders**, and 2 pieces $1\frac{1}{2}$" x $11\frac{1}{2}$" for **side inner borders**.

4. **From assorted plaids:** ◩
   - Cut 1 **medium square** $3\frac{1}{2}$" x $3\frac{1}{2}$" from 1 plaid for dog coat.
   - Cut 1 rectangle $1\frac{3}{4}$" x 7" from 1 plaid for **bow**.
   - Cut $2\frac{1}{4}$"w assorted pieces that vary in length from $2\frac{1}{2}$" to 5" for **outer border pieces**.

ASSEMBLING THE PILLOW TOP

*Follow **Piecing and Pressing**, page 146, to make pillow top.*

1. To make triangle-squares, place white and black **large squares** right sides together. Referring to **Fig. 1**, follow Steps 1 - 3 of **Making Triangle-Squares**, page 146, to draw a grid of 4 squares $2^3/8$" x $2^3/8$". Referring to **Fig. 2** for sewing directions, follow Steps 4 - 6 of **Making Triangle-Squares**, page 146, to make a total of 8 **triangle-squares** (you will need 6 and have 2 left over).

Fig. 1   **Fig. 2**

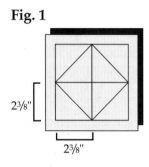 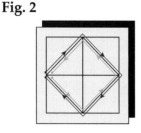

triangle-square (make 8)

2. Making 1 of each unit, follow Steps 2 - 10 of **Assembling the Wall Hanging Top (Scottie Dog Blocks)**, page 98, for **Scottie Wall Hanging** to make 1 **Scottie Dog Block**.
3. Sew **top**, **bottom**, and then **side inner borders** to **Scottie Dog Block**.
4. For outer border, refer to **Pillow Top Diagram** and sew **outer border pieces** together to make 2 **top/bottom outer borders** $2^1/4$" x $11^1/2$" and 2 **side borders** $2^1/4$" x $14^1/2$". Sew **top**, **bottom**, and then **side outer borders** to inner borders to complete **Pillow Top**.

COMPLETING THE PILLOW

1. Follow **Quilting**, page 151, to mark, layer, and quilt. For quilting on **Scottie Pillow Top**, refer to **Scottie Wall Hanging Quilting Diagram**, page 101.
2. Follow Steps 5 and 6 of **Completing the Wall Hanging**, page 100, for **Scottie Wall Hanging** to make and attach **bow** and button to pillow top.
3. Follow **Pillow Finishing**, page 157, to complete pillow with a 3" ruffle.

Pillow Top Diagram

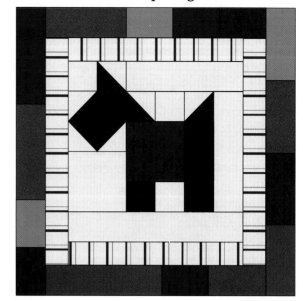

SCOTTIE DOG JUMPER

SUPPLIES

Yardage is based on 45"w fabric.

 $1/2$ yd of red plaid
 $1/2$ yd of blue and white stripe
 scrap of black

You will also need:

 a jumper
 $1/8$" cord for piping
 paper-backed fusible web
 red and black thread
 covered button kit

MAKING THE JUMPER

1. Wash, dry, and press jumper, fabrics, and cord.
2. Cut 1 plaid piece $8^1/2$" x 10" for pocket and 1 striped square $6^1/2$" x $6^1/2$" for pocket center.
3. Press all edges of pocket piece $1/2$" to wrong side; press 1 short edge (top) $1^1/2$" to wrong side again to make a square $7^1/2$" x $7^1/2$".
4. Press edges of pocket center $1/4$" to wrong side. Center pocket center, right side up, on right side of pocket. Topstitch along pressed edges of pocket center.
5. Referring to **Pocket Diagram**, use **Scottie Dog** and **Bow Tie Patterns** and follow **Preparing Appliqué Pieces**, page 148, and **Satin Stitch Appliqué**, page 148, to appliqué pieces to pocket center.
6. Position pocket on jumper and topstitch pocket in place along side and bottom edges.

7. (**Note:** Follow Steps 7 - 12 to pipe and bind neck edge and each armhole edge.) Measure around neck edge and add 1". Cut 1 bias strip 1½"w of striped fabric, 1 bias strip 2½"w of plaid fabric, and 1 length of cord the determined measurement.

8. For piping, lay cord along center of striped bias strip on wrong side of fabric; fold strip over cord. With zipper foot, machine baste along length of strip close to cord. Trim seam allowance to ½".

9. Matching raw edge of piping to neck edge and beginning 1" from end of piping, baste piping to right side of jumper.

10. Remove approximately 3" of stitching at 1 end of piping; fold fabric away from cord. Trim remaining end of piping so that cord ends meet exactly. Fold short edge of piping fabric ½" to wrong side; fold fabric back over area where cord ends meet. Baste remainder of piping to neck edge close to cord.

11. For binding, press 1 short edge of plaid bias strip ½" to wrong side. Matching wrong sides, press strip in half lengthwise. On wrong side of jumper, place pressed short edge of strip at a seam and match long raw edge of binding to neck edge. Using a ¼" seam allowance, sew binding to neck edge.

12. Press binding over neck edge to right side of jumper, covering raw edge of piping. Topstitch along folded edge of binding next to piping.

13. For bow, cut 1 plaid bias strip 3" x 36". Matching right sides, press strip in half lengthwise. Trim ends of strip diagonally. Sew raw edges together, leaving 1 short edge open for turning. Cut corners diagonally, turn right side out, and press. Blindstitch opening closed. Tie into a bow and use a safety pin on wrong side of jumper to pin bow to jumper.

14. Follow manufacturer's instructions to cover buttons with matching plaid. Replace buttons on jumper with covered buttons.

Pocket Diagram

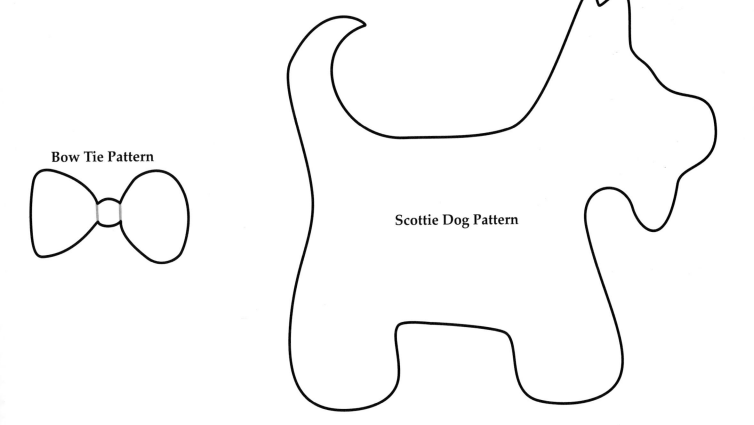

Bow Tie Pattern

Scottie Dog Pattern

LOG CABIN COLLECTION

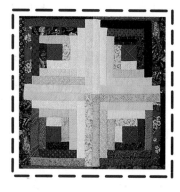

An easy pattern with an enduring popularity, the Log Cabin design dates back to Civil War days when Americans became fascinated with President Abraham Lincoln's humble beginnings in a cabin. Quilters were delighted with the dramatic effects they could create with the pattern using scraps of wool, calicoes, and shirting prints. As dozens of variations developed, the pattern even merited its own quilting category at state fairs. Traditional Log Cabin blocks begin with a center square of red fabric to represent the fireplace that was always the heart of the home. To make our Sunshine and Shadows variation even easier, we sewed the "logs" around the center square and then rotary cut them to an exact fit — so there are no tiny pieces to handle! Our nifty grid method makes the Sawtooth border a breeze to piece, too.

Bring the rustic beauty of our Log Cabin quilt to your entire room with these handsome accessories. To showcase our Sunshine and Shadows pattern, a design that brings to mind the warmth of hearth and home, we created this eye-catching wall hanging (below). The striking arrangement of the quilt blocks and its quaint appliquéd design makes it the perfect mantel accent. (Opposite) Columns of Log Cabin quilt blocks create an unusual but easy window treatment — indoor shutters! To complete your collection, add a comfy throw pillow featuring an appliquéd cabin block with a patchwork border.

LOG CABIN QUILT

SKILL LEVEL: 1 2 3 4 5
BLOCK SIZE: 10" x 10"
QUILT SIZE: 91" x 111"

YARDAGE REQUIREMENTS

Yardage is based on 45"w fabric.

- ¼ yd of red
- 3¼ yds **total** of assorted dark prints
- 3 yds **total** of assorted light prints
- 3⅝ yds of tan print for narrow borders
- 1 yd of dark red for pieced border
- 1⅛ yds of grey for pieced border
- 3⅝ yds of floral print for outer border
  8¼ yds for backing
  1 yd for binding
  120" x 120" batting

CUTTING OUT THE PIECES

All measurements include a ¼" seam allowance. Follow Rotary Cutting, page 144, to cut fabric.

1. **From red:**
   - Cut 3 selvage-to-selvage strips 2½"w. From these strips, cut a total of 48 squares 2½" x 2½" for **center squares.**
2. **From assorted dark prints:**
   - Cut a total of 70 selvage-to-selvage **strips** 1½"w.
3. **From assorted light prints:**
   - Cut a total of 60 selvage-to-selvage **strips** 1½"w.
4. **From tan print:**
   - Cut 2 lengthwise strips 3" x 69" for **first (inner) top/bottom borders.**
   - Cut 2 lengthwise strips 3" x 89" for **first side borders.**
   - Cut 2 lengthwise strips 3" x 94" for **third top/bottom borders.**
   - Cut 2 lengthwise strips 3" x 114" for **third side borders.**
5. **From dark red:**
   - Cut 2 **rectangles** 19" x 31" for triangle-squares.
6. **From grey:**
   - Cut 2 **rectangles** 19" x 31" for triangle-squares.
   - Cut 4 squares 5½" x 5½" for **border corner squares.**
7. **From floral print:**
   - Cut 2 lengthwise strips 5½" x 94" for **fourth top/bottom borders.**
   - Cut 2 lengthwise strips 5½" by 114" for **fourth side borders.**

ASSEMBLING THE QUILT TOP

*Follow **Piecing and Pressing**, page 146, to make quilt top.*

1. Place 1 light print **strip** on 1 **center square** with right sides together and matching 1 long raw edge of strip with 1 raw edge of square. Stitch as shown in **Fig. 1**. Trim strip even with square (**Fig. 2**); open and press (**Fig. 3**).

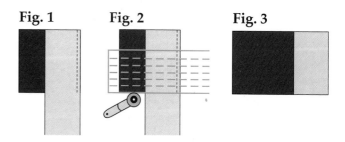

Fig. 1   **Fig. 2**   **Fig. 3**

2. Turning center square ¼ turn to the left, use a different light print **strip** and repeat Step 1 to add the next "log" as shown in **Figs. 4 - 6**.

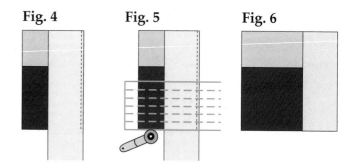

Fig. 4   **Fig. 5**   **Fig. 6**

3. Repeat Step 2, adding 2 different dark print **strips** to remaining 2 sides of center square (**Fig. 7**).

Fig. 7

4. Continue to add **strips**, alternating 2 light and 2 dark strips until there are 4 strips on each side of center square to complete **Block**.

Block (make 48)

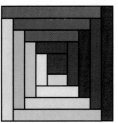

5. Repeat Steps 1 - 4 to make 48 **Blocks**.
6. Assemble 6 **Blocks** as shown to make **Row**. Make 8 **Rows**.

Row (make 8)

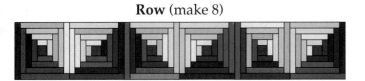

7. Referring to **Quilt Top Diagram**, page 110, assemble **Rows** to complete center section of quilt top.
8. Follow **Adding Mitered Borders**, page 150, to add **first border**.
9. To make triangle-squares, place 1 dark red and 1 grey **rectangle** right sides together. Referring to **Fig. 8**, follow Steps 1 - 3 of **Making Triangle-Squares**, page 146, to mark a grid of 15 squares $5\frac{7}{8}$" x $5\frac{7}{8}$". Referring to **Fig. 9** for sewing directions, follow Steps 4 - 6 of **Making Triangle-Squares**, page 146, to complete 30 triangle-squares. Repeat with remaining **rectangles** to make a total of 60 **triangle-squares**.

Fig. 8

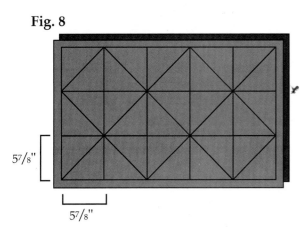

$5\frac{7}{8}$"

$5\frac{7}{8}$"

Fig. 9

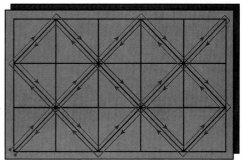

triangle-square (make 60)

10. Assemble 17 **triangle-squares** as shown to make **Second Side Border**. Make 2 **Second Side Borders**.

Second Side Border (make 2)

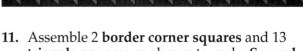

11. Assemble 2 **border corner squares** and 13 **triangle-squares** as shown to make **Second Top/Bottom Border**. Make 2 **Second Top/Bottom Borders**.

Second Top/Bottom Border (make 2)

12. Sew **Second Side Borders**, then **Second Top/Bottom Borders** to center section of quilt top.
13. Assemble **third** and **fourth borders** as shown to make **Border Unit**. Make 2 **Top/Bottom Border Units** and 2 **Side Border Units**.

Border Unit

14. Follow **Adding Mitered Borders**, page 150, to attach **Border Units** to center section of quilt top to complete **Quilt Top**.

COMPLETING THE QUILT

1. Follow **Quilting**, page 151, and **Quilting Diagram** and use **Wave Quilting Pattern**, page 114, and **Small** and **Large Cable Quilting Patterns**, page 115, to mark, layer, and quilt.
2. Cut a 36" square of binding fabric. Follow **Making Continuous Bias Strip Binding**, page 155, to make approximately 12 yds of 2 1/2"w bias binding.
3. Follow **Attaching Binding with Mitered Corners**, page 155, to attach binding to quilt.

Quilting Diagram

Quilt Top Diagram

LOG CABIN WALL HANGING

SKILL LEVEL: 1 2 3 **4** 5
BLOCK SIZE: 7" x 7"
WALL HANGING SIZE: 43" x 43"

YARDAGE REQUIREMENTS

Yardage is based on 45"w fabric.

- 1/8 yd of red
- 1 1/4 yds **total** of assorted dark prints
- 7/8 yd **total** of assorted cream prints
- 3/4 yd **total** of assorted tan prints
- scraps for appliqués
  3 yds for backing and hanging sleeve
  3/4 yd for binding
  45" x 60" batting

You will also need:
  paper-backed fusible web
  transparent monofilament thread for appliqué

CUTTING OUT THE PIECES

All measurements include a 1/4" seam allowance. Follow Rotary Cutting, page 144, to cut fabric.

1. **From red:**
   - Cut 2 selvage-to-selvage strips 1 1/2"w. From these strips, cut 32 squares 1 1/2" x 1 1/2" for **center squares**.

2. **From assorted dark prints:**
   - Cut a total of 27 selvage-to-selvage **strips** 1 1/2"w.

3. **From assorted cream prints:**
   - Cut 1 square 14 1/2" x 14 1/2" from 1 print for **center block**.
   - Cut a total of 9 selvage-to-selvage **strips** 1 1/2"w.

4. **From assorted tan prints:**
   - Cut a total of 14 selvage-to-selvage **strips** 1 1/2"w.

5. **From scraps:**
   - Cut 4 bias strips 1/2" x 13" and 4 bias strips 1/2" x 7" for **vines**.
   - Referring to photo, follow **Preparing Appliqué Pieces**, page 148, to cut the following number of pieces from **Appliqué Patterns**, pages 114 and 115:
     - Flowers — 14
     - Flower Centers — 14
     - Leaves — 28
     - Vine Heart — 16
     - Roof — 1
     - Gable — 1
     - House Heart — 1
     - House Front — 1 rectangle 4" x 6"

House Side — 1 rectangle 5" x 6"
Door — 1 rectangle 1 1/2" x 4"
Chimney — 1 rectangle 1" x 1 3/4"
Windows — 2 rectangles 1 1/2" x 2"

ASSEMBLING THE WALL HANGING TOP

*Follow **Piecing and Pressing**, page 146, to make wall hanging top.*

1. Refer to **Wall Hanging Top Diagram**, page 112, and follow **Almost Invisible Appliqué**, page 149, to appliqué house pieces only to **center block**.

2. Follow Steps 1 - 4 of **Assembling the Quilt Top** for **Log Cabin Quilt**, page 108, to make 12 **Block A's** as shown using cream and dark strips and 20 **Block B's** as shown using tan and dark strips. (*Note*: The blocks for the **Log Cabin Wall Hanging** use smaller center squares than those in the **Log Cabin Quilt** and have 3 strips on each side of the center square instead of 4.)

Block A (make 12)   **Block B** (make 20)

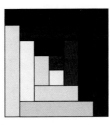 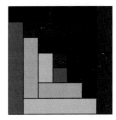

3. Assemble 6 **Block B's** as shown to make **Unit 1**. Make 2 **Unit 1's**.

Unit 1 (make 2)

4. Assemble 2 **Block B's** and 4 **Block A's** as shown to make **Unit 2**. Make 2 **Unit 2's**.

Unit 2 (make 2)

5. Assemble 2 **Block B's** and 2 **Block A's** as shown to make **Unit 3**. Make 2 **Unit 3's**.

Unit 3 (make 2)

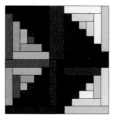

6. Referring to **Wall Hanging Top Diagram**, assemble **Unit 1's**, **Unit 2's**, **Unit 3's**, and **center block**.

7. Referring to **Wall Hanging Top Diagram**, hand baste **vines** in place; fuse remaining appliqué pieces in place. Follow **Almost Invisible Appliqué**, page 149, to appliqué **vines**, **flowers**, **leaves**, and **vine hearts** to complete **Wall Hanging Top**.

COMPLETING THE WALL HANGING

1. Follow **Quilting**, page 151, and **Quilting Diagram** to mark, layer, and quilt.
2. Follow **Making a Hanging Sleeve**, page 157, to attach hanging sleeve to wall hanging.
3. Cut a 27" square of binding fabric. Follow **Making Continuous Bias Strip Binding**, page 155, to make approximately 5¼ yds of 2½"w bias binding.
4. Follow **Attaching Binding with Mitered Corners**, page 155, to attach binding to wall hanging.

Quilting Diagram

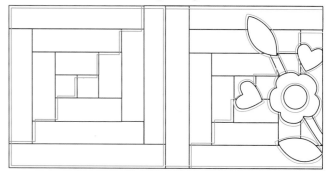

Wall Hanging Top Diagram

112

LOG CABIN PILLOW

PILLOW SIZE: 18" x 18"

YARDAGE REQUIREMENTS
Yardage is based on 45"w fabric.

☐ 12½" x 12½" square of cream print fabric

■ scraps for appliqués and borders
21½" x 21½" square for pillow top backing
19" x 19" square for pillow back
3" x 76" bias strip (pieced if necessary)
for welting

You will also need:
paper-backed fusible web
21½" x 21½" batting
2⅛ yds of ½" cord for welting
transparent monofilament thread for appliqué
polyester fiberfill

MAKING THE PILLOW
1. Follow **Preparing Appliqué Pieces**, page 148, to cut out house shapes listed in Step 5 of **Cutting Out the Pieces** for **Log Cabin Wall Hanging**, page 111.
2. Refer to **Pillow Top Diagram** and follow **Almost Invisible Appliqué**, page 149, to appliqué house pieces to 12½" x 12½" square.
3. For inner borders, cut scraps into 2"w strips that vary in length from 3" to 8". Referring to **Pillow Top Diagram**, assemble strips, trim to fit, and sew to sides, then top and bottom of 12½" x 12½" square. Repeat for outer borders.
4. Follow **Quilting**, page 151, to layer and quilt in the ditch around house and border pieces.
5. Follow **Pillow Finishing**, page 157, to complete pillow with welting.

Pillow Top Diagram

LOG CABIN SHUTTERS

SHUTTER SIZE: 13" x 73" each

Our shutters fit a 72"l window. For smaller or larger windows, adjust size accordingly.

YARDAGE REQUIREMENTS
Yardage is based on 45"w fabric.

■ ⅛ yd of red

◧ 1 yd **total** of assorted dark prints

◪ 1 yd **total** of assorted light prints

▩ ½ yd of light print for borders
2¼ yds for backing and hanging sleeves
1 yd for binding
72" x 90" batting

CUTTING OUT THE PIECES
All measurements include a ¼" seam allowance. Follow Rotary Cutting, page 144, to cut fabric.

1. **From red:** ■
   - Cut 1 selvage-to-selvage strip 2½"w. From this strip, cut 14 squares 2½" x 2½" for **center squares**.
2. **From assorted dark prints:** ◧
   - Cut a total of 22 selvage-to-selvage **strips** 1½"w.
3. **From assorted light prints:** ◪
   - Cut a total of 18 selvage-to-selvage **strips** 1½"w.
4. **From light print for borders:** ▩
   - Cut a total of 10 selvage-to-selvage strips 1½"w for **borders**.

ASSEMBLING THE SHUTTER TOPS
Follow Piecing and Pressing, page 146, to make shutter tops.

1. Follow Steps 1 - 4 of **Assembling the Quilt Top** for **Log Cabin Quilt**, page 108, to make 14 **Blocks**.
2. Referring to photo, assemble 7 **Blocks** to make center section of shutter top. Make 2 center sections.
3. Piecing strips as necessary, follow **Adding Squared Borders**, page 150, to add **borders** to complete each shutter top.

COMPLETING THE SHUTTERS

1. Follow **Quilting**, page 151, and **Quilting Diagram** to mark, layer, and quilt each shutter.
2. Follow **Making a Hanging Sleeve**, page 157, to attach a hanging sleeve to each shutter.
3. Cut a 36" square of binding fabric. Follow **Making Continuous Bias Strip Binding**, page 155, to make approximately 10½ yds of 2½"w bias binding.
4. Follow **Attaching Binding with Mitered Corners**, page 155, to attach binding to each shutter.

Quilting Diagram

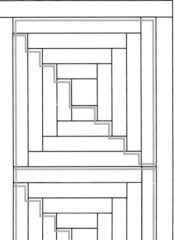

Leaf

Wave Quilting Pattern

Vine Heart

Flower

Flower Center

Roof

Gable

House Heart

Large Cable Quilting Pattern

Small Cable Quilting Pattern

LeMOYNE STAR

The LeMoyne Star, one of the most esteemed diamond-based designs, was named in honor of French-Canadian naval officers Pierre LeMoyne, sieur d'Iberville, and his brother, Jean Baptiste LeMoyne, sieur d'Bienville. Their explorations of the lower Mississippi River and Southern coast ultimately led to the French settlement of the land we now call Louisiana. The pattern's name was often misunderstood to be Lemon Star because of the colorful accent of the region. For our jewel-toned variation of the traditional design, we used fast, accurate rotary cutting methods to cut the star and setting pieces. An easy-to-add border provides dramatic flair — and an opportunity for experienced stitchers to delight in ornate quilting that will make their work a blue-ribbon beauty!

116

LeMOYNE STAR QUILT

SKILL LEVEL: 1 2 3 4 5
BLOCK SIZE: 7¼" x 7¼"
QUILT SIZE: 88" x 98"

YARDAGE REQUIREMENTS

Yardage is based on 45"w fabric.

 5 yds of dark blue

2¾ yds **total** of assorted solids for stars (our quilt uses 12 different solids)

2¼ yds of light blue

1⅝ yds of cream
8 yds for backing
¾ yd for binding
120" x 120" batting

CUTTING OUT THE PIECES

All measurements include a ¼" seam allowance. Follow
***Rotary Cutting**, page 144, to cut fabric.*

1. **From dark blue:**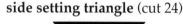

   - Cut 2 lengthwise strips 10½" x 91" for **top/bottom outer borders**.
   - Cut 2 lengthwise strips 10½" x 81" for **side outer borders**.
   - Cut 2 selvage-to-selvage strips 11½"w. From these strips, cut 6 squares 11½" x 11½". Cut squares twice diagonally to make a total of 24 **side setting triangles** (you will need 22 and have 2 left over).

   side setting triangle (cut 24)

   - Cut 6 selvage-to-selvage strips 7¾"w. From these strips, cut a total of 30 **setting squares** 7¾" x 7¾".

   setting square (cut 30)

   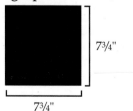

   - Cut 2 squares 6" x 6". Cut each square once diagonally to make 4 **corner setting triangles**.

   corner setting triangle (cut 4)

   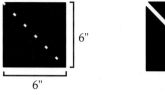

2. **From assorted solids:**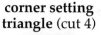

   - Cut a total of 42 selvage-to-selvage **strips** 2"w. (Each strip will make 1 star.)

3. **From light blue:**

   - Cut 2 lengthwise strips 3" x 76" for **side inner borders**.
   - Cut 2 lengthwise strips 3" x 71" for **top/bottom inner borders**.

4. **From cream:**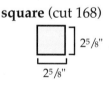

   - Cut 5 selvage-to-selvage strips 4¼"w. From these strips, cut 42 squares 4¼" x 4¼". Cut squares twice diagonally to make a total of 168 **triangles**.

   triangle (cut 168)

   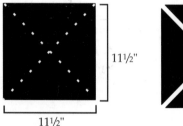

   - Cut 11 selvage-to-selvage strips 2⅝"w. From these strips, cut a total of 168 **squares** 2⅝" x 2⅝".

   square (cut 168)

ASSEMBLING THE QUILT TOP

*Follow **Piecing and Pressing**, page 146, to make quilt top.*

1. Referring to **Fig. 1**, align the 45° marking (shown in pink) on the rotary cutting ruler along the lower edge of 1 **strip**. Cut along right side of ruler to cut 1 end of each solid **strip** at a 45° angle.

   Fig. 1

   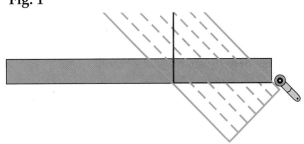

2. Turn cut **strip** 180° on mat and align the 45° marking on the rotary cutting ruler along the lower edge of the strip. Align the previously cut 45° edge with the 2" marking on the ruler. Cut strip at 2" intervals as shown in **Fig. 2** to cut a total of 8 **diamonds** from each **strip**.

   Fig. 2

   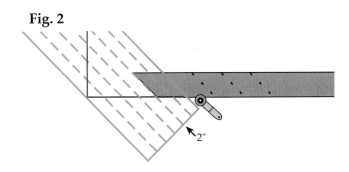

3. (*Note:* Follow Steps 3 - 6 to make each Star Block. Make a total of 42 Star Blocks. Refer to **Working with Diamond Shapes**, page 147, when assembling Star Blocks.) Assemble 2 matching **diamonds** as shown to make **Unit 1**. (Arrow indicates stitching direction.) Make 4 **Unit 1's**.

   Unit 1 (make 4)

   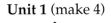

4. Assemble 2 **Unit 1's** to make **Unit 2**. Make 2 **Unit 2's**.

   Unit 2 (make 2)

   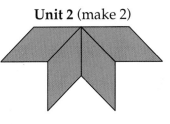

5. Assemble 2 **Unit 2's** to make **Unit 3**.

   Unit 3 (make 1)

   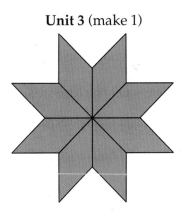

6. Assemble **Unit 3**, 4 **squares**, and 4 **triangles** to make **Star Block**.

   Star Block

   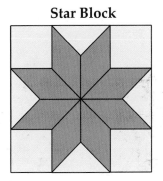

7. Follow **Assembly Diagram**, page 120, to sew **Star Blocks**, **setting squares**, **side setting triangles**, and **corner setting triangles** into rows; sew rows together to complete center section of quilt top.

8. Follow **Adding Squared Borders**, page 150, and **Quilt Top Diagram**, page 120, to sew **side**, then **top** and **bottom inner borders** to center section of quilt top. Add **side**, then **top** and **bottom outer borders** to complete **Quilt Top**.

COMPLETING THE QUILT

1. Follow Step 3 of **Using Quilting Stencils and Templates**, page 152, and use **Feather** and **Heart Template Patterns** to make a pattern for feather quilting. Follow **Quilting**, page 151, and **Quilting Diagram** and use **Diamond Wave** and **Feather Wreath Patterns**, pages 122 and 123, to mark, layer, and quilt.
2. Follow **Making Straight-Grain Binding**, page 155, to make 2¹/₂"w binding.
3. Follow **Attaching Binding with Overlapped Corners**, page 156, to attach binding to quilt.

Assembly Diagram

Quilt Top Diagram

120

Quilting Diagram

Feather Template Pattern

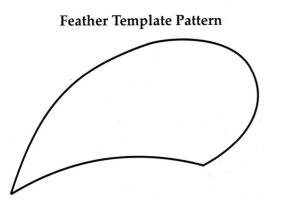

Heart Template Pattern

Diamond Wave Pattern

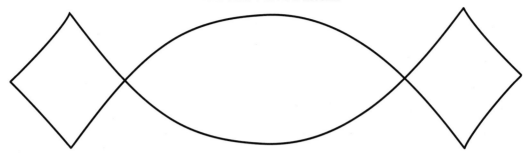

QUICK TIP

ORGANIZING YOUR QUILTMAKING

Using our quick methods makes quiltmaking faster and easier, as well as more enjoyable and satisfying. Organizing your supplies and workspace will help you to accomplish even more during the time you have to devote to quiltmaking. Try the following suggestions:

- *If you don't have a sewing room, use a portable, easily stored container to keep all your tools and supplies in one place. You can use laundry baskets that will stack in a closet, under-bed storage boxes, or even a cardboard box stored under a skirted table.*

- *Store all the materials for an individual project in a smaller box or other container. Include the fabric, thread, and other supplies, as well as the project instructions and any special tools you may need. Label the individual project boxes.*

- *Before putting a project away, label any pieces that may be difficult to identify later. Make notes on your instructions (use self-stick notes if you don't want to write in the book) that will help you quickly pick up where you left off.*

- *Never put away a project when you're having a problem. Rip out mistakes and work out problems before you stop working so that you'll look forward to getting back to the project.*

- *Invest in tools and supplies that will make your work easier. Trying to work with poor-quality tools or the wrong tool for the job will only lead to frustration and dissatisfaction.*

- *Choose projects carefully. Alternate quilts that stretch your time and abilities with simpler, smaller projects like wall hangings or lap quilts. Try a few fast, fun projects (like our Amish Sweatshirt, page 55) that you can finish quickly. The satisfaction of finishing one project is always good motivation to finish another!*

Feather Wreath Pattern

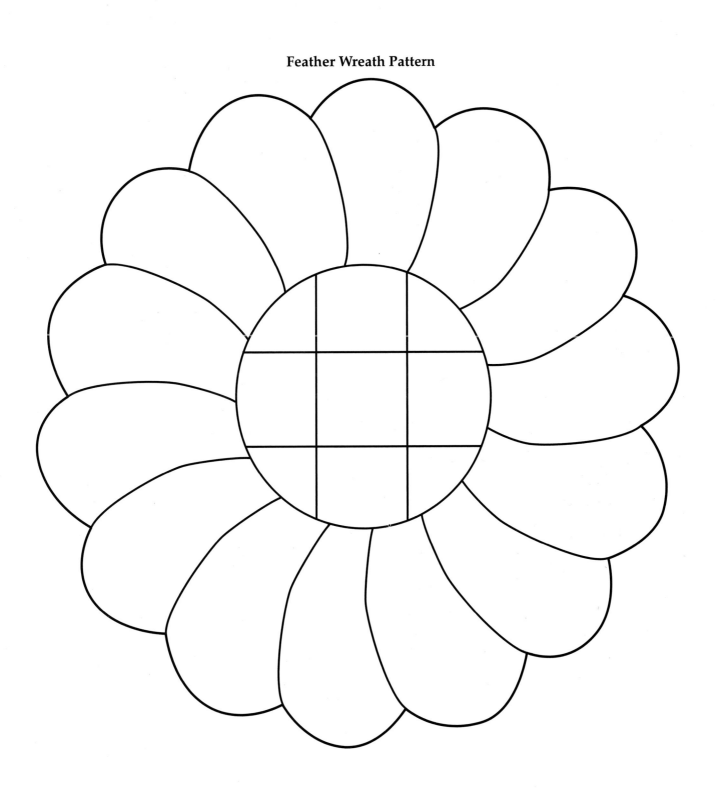

OCEAN WAVES

A crisp blue and white color scheme perfectly complements the flowing design of this pretty Ocean Waves quilt. To reproduce the classic nautical pattern, we used rotary cutting for all of the pieces — even on portions of the prairie-point edging! A simple grid method makes piecing the triangles easier and more accurate than traditional quiltmaking, and with only two fabrics to work with, you'll finish in a fraction of the time. A combination of outline and grid quilting completes this lovely showpiece.

OCEAN WAVES QUILT

SKILL LEVEL: 1 2 3 4 5
BLOCK SIZE: 8" x 8"
QUILT SIZE: 84" x 98"

Our quick-and-easy prairie point instructions allow you to make continuous lengths of overlapping prairie points. The overlapping prairie points will look slightly different than the single prairie points featured on the antique quilt in the photograph.

YARDAGE REQUIREMENTS
Yardage is based on 45"w fabric.

☐ 7³/₈ yds of white

▨ 6 yds of blue

▨ 1³/₄ yds for prairie point edging
8 yds for backing
90" x 108" batting

CUTTING OUT THE PIECES
All measurements include a ¹/₄" seam allowance. Follow Rotary Cutting, page 144, to cut fabric.

1. **From white:** ☐
    *   Cut 2 lengthwise strips 3¹/₂" x 90" for **side inner borders**.
    *   Cut 2 lengthwise strips 3¹/₂" x 74" for **top/bottom inner borders**.
    *   Cut 11 **rectangles** 18" x 22" for triangle-squares.
    *   Cut 2 selvage-to-selvage strips 9¹/₄"w. From these strips, cut a total of 5 squares 9¹/₄" x 9¹/₄". Cut squares twice diagonally to make 20 **large triangles** (you will need 18 and have 2 left over).

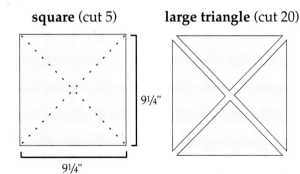

square (cut 5)   **large triangle** (cut 20)

9¹/₄"

9¹/₄"

*   Cut 10 selvage-to-selvage strips 2⁷/₈"w. From these strips, cut a total of 138 squares 2⁷/₈" x 2⁷/₈". Cut squares once diagonally to make 276 **triangles**.

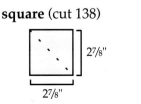

square (cut 138)   **triangle** (cut 276)

2⁷/₈"

2⁷/₈"

*   Cut 6 selvage-to-selvage strips 6¹/₈"w. From these strips, cut a total of 31 **squares** 6¹/₈" x 6¹/₈".

2. **From blue:** ▨
    *   Cut 2 lengthwise strips 3¹/₂" x 102" for **side outer borders**.
    *   Cut 2 lengthwise strips 3¹/₂" x 86" for **top/bottom outer borders**.
    *   Cut 11 **rectangles** 18" x 22" for triangle-squares.
    *   Cut 10 selvage-to-selvage strips 2⁷/₈"w. From these strips, cut a total of 134 squares 2⁷/₈" x 2⁷/₈". Cut squares once diagonally to make 268 **triangles**.

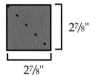

square (cut 134)   **triangle** (cut 268)

2⁷/₈"

2⁷/₈"

3. **From prairie point edging fabric:**
    *   Cut 10 selvage-to-selvage strips 6"w. From these strips, cut 18 **long pieces** 6" x 19¹/₂" and 4 **short pieces** 6" x 10¹/₂".

ASSEMBLING THE QUILT TOP
Follow Piecing and Pressing, page 146, to make quilt top.

1. To make triangle-squares, place 1 white and 1 blue **rectangle** right sides together. Referring to **Fig. 1**, follow Steps 1 - 3 of **Making Triangle-Squares**, page 146, to draw a grid of 42 squares 2⁷/₈" x 2⁷/₈". Referring to **Fig. 2** for sewing directions, follow Steps 4 - 6 of **Making Triangle-Squares**, page 146, to complete a total of 84 triangle-squares. Repeat with remaining **rectangles** to make a total of 924 **triangle-squares** (you will need 912 and have 12 left over).

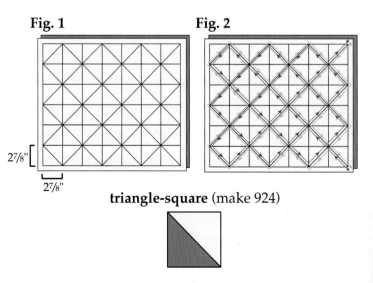

Fig. 1   **Fig. 2**

2⁷/₈"

2⁷/₈"

triangle-square (make 924)

2. Assemble 4 **triangle-squares** as shown to make **Unit 1**. Make 160 **Unit 1's**.

Unit 1 (make 160)

3. Assemble 4 **Unit 1's** as shown to make **Block A**. Make 20 **Block A's**.

Block A (make 20)

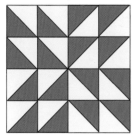

4. Assemble 2 **Unit 1's** as shown to make **Block B**. Make 14 **Block B's**.

Block B (make 14)

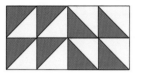

5. Assemble 4 **Unit 1's** as shown to make **Block C**. Make 12 **Block C's**.

Block C (make 12)

6. Assemble 1 **triangle-square** and 2 **triangles** as shown to make **Unit 3**. Make 84 **Unit 3's**.
   Assemble 1 **triangle-square** and 2 **triangles** as shown to make **Unit 4**. Make 80 **Unit 4's**.

Unit 3 (make 84)   **Unit 4** (make 80)

7. Assemble 2 **Unit 3's**, 2 **Unit 4's**, and 1 **square** as shown to make **Block D**. Make 31 **Block D's**.

Block D (make 31)

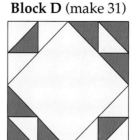

8. Assemble 1 **Unit 4**, 1 **Unit 3**, and 1 **large triangle** as shown to make **Block E**. Make 18 **Block E's**.

Block E (make 18)

9. Assemble 2 **Unit 1's**, 4 **Block E's** and 3 **Block B's** as shown to make **Row A**. Make 2 **Row A's**.

Row A (make 2)

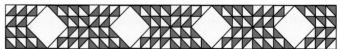

10. Assemble 2 **Block E's**, 4 **Block A's**, and 3 **Block D's** as shown to make **Row B**. Make 5 **Row B's**.

Row B (make 5)

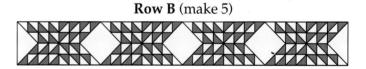

11. Assemble 2 **Block B's**, 4 **Block D's**, and 3 **Block C's** as shown to make **Row C**. Make 4 **Row C's**.

Row C (make 4)

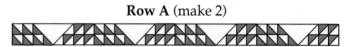

12. Referring to **Quilt Top Diagram**, page 129, assemble **Rows** to complete center section of quilt top.

13. Follow **Adding Mitered Borders**, page 150, to attach **inner borders** to center section of quilt top.

14. Assemble 1 **triangle-square** and 2 **triangles** as shown to make **Unit 5**. Make 108 **Unit 5's**.

Unit 5 (make 108)

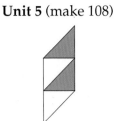

15. Assemble 24 **Unit 5's** and 1 **Unit 3** as shown to make **Top/Bottom Pieced Border**. Make 2 **Top/Bottom Pieced Borders**.

Top/Bottom Pieced Border (make 2)

16. Assemble 30 **Unit 5's** and 1 **Unit 3** as shown to make **Side Pieced Border**. Make 2 **Side Pieced Borders**.

Side Pieced Border (make 2)

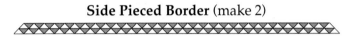

17. Sew **Pieced Borders** to top, bottom, and sides of center section of quilt top, beginning and ending seams exactly ¼" from each corner of quilt top and backstitching at beginning and end of stitching.

18. Fold 1 corner of quilt top diagonally with right sides together, matching outer edges of borders as shown in **Fig. 3**. Beginning at point where previous seams ended, stitch to outer corner. Repeat with remaining corners.

Fig. 3

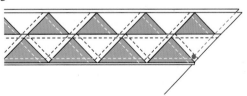

19. Follow **Adding Mitered Borders**, page 150, to attach **outer borders** to complete **Quilt Top**.

MAKING PRAIRIE POINT EDGING

1. Place 1 **long piece** wrong side up. Referring to **Fig. 1**, mark a line along center of piece. Beginning at left edge above the center line, mark lines 3" apart. Beginning 1½" from the left edge below the center line, mark lines 3" apart.

Fig. 1

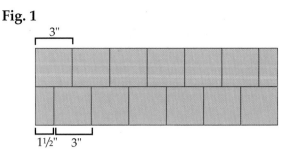

2. Referring to **Fig. 2**, use scissors to trim away 1½"w sections and to cut along 3" drawn lines up to the center line.

Fig. 2

3. Referring to **Fig. 3**, press first "square" to right of center line in half diagonally once; press in half diagonally again and pin to form prairie point (**Fig. 4**).

Fig. 3   **Fig. 4**

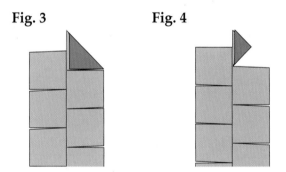

4. Press first "square" to left of center line in half diagonally once (**Fig. 5**). Press prairie point on right to the left along the center line; press second fold of triangle over first prairie point and pin to form second prairie point (**Fig. 6**).

Fig. 5   **Fig. 6**

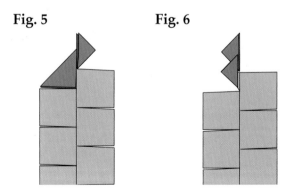

5. Alternating from 1 side of the center line to the other, repeat Step 4 until all squares are folded to form prairie points. Stitch a scant 1/4" from base of prairie points to complete **Prairie Point Unit**.

Prairie Point Unit

6. Repeat Steps 1 - 5 with remaining **long** and **short pieces** to complete 18 **Long Prairie Point Units** and 4 **Short Prairie Point Units**.

COMPLETING THE QUILT

1. Follow **Quilting**, page 151, and **Quilting Diagram** to mark, layer, and quilt to within 1" of edges of quilt. Trim backing and batting even with quilt top.
2. Fold backing away from edges of quilt. Using 1 **Short Prairie Point Unit** and 4 **Long Prairie Point Units** for top and bottom edges and 1 **Short Prairie Point Unit** and 5 **Long Prairie Point Units** for each side edge, pin **Prairie Point Units** on right side along each edge of quilt top, overlapping and easing Units as

necessary. Sew prairie points to quilt top and batting. Press prairie points away from center of quilt top.
3. Finger press edge of backing 1/4" to wrong side. Covering raw edge of prairie points and stitching, blindstitch backing in place.

Quilting Diagram

Quilt Top Diagram

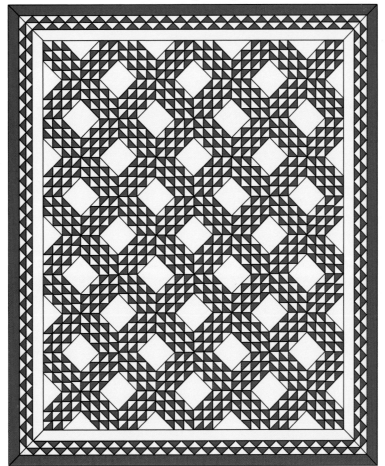

WILD ROSE COLLECTION

Romance blooms to life in this fabulously feminine quilt! The fanciful nosegays and beribboned borders look lovely on a field of delicate prints. In years past, appliquéd quilts such as this were considered "best quilts" because of the time and attention to detail taken in making them. They were saved for special occasions, when everyday quilts were packed away and these glorious showpieces were displayed for guests to admire. For our original design, we saved time by rotary cutting the pieces for our Square-Within-a-Square variation blocks. And the machine satin stitching we used to appliqué the Wild Rose bouquets will thrill accomplished quilters because it eliminates traditional (and slower) hand sewing! With our coordinating pillow shams and other accessories, you can create a set that will become a treasured heirloom.

You'll be enchanted by these charming additions to our genteel collection. Made using fabrics from our quilt, all of the matching accessories are easy to embellish with fused-on appliqués and machine satin stitching. The rose-trimmed table topper is a pretty way to complete your bedroom decor. (Opposite) Appliquéd blooms edged with blanket stitching, along with buttons, lace, and ribbon, are sweet accents for a purchased nightgown.

WILD ROSE BOUQUET QUILT

SKILL LEVEL: 1 2 3 4 5
BLOCK SIZE: 10½" x 10½"
QUILT SIZE: 84" x 99"

YARDAGE REQUIREMENTS

Yardage is based on 45"w fabric.

- [ ] 3¾ yds of white print
- [ ] 3 yds of mauve print
- [ ] 1⅝ yds of mauve/blue floral
- [ ] 1½ yds of pink print
- [ ] 1½ yds of light blue print
- [ ] 1 yd of blue
- [ ] ¾ yd of green
- [ ] ½ yd of mauve
- [ ] ¼ yd of dark mauve print

  8 yds for backing
  1 yd for binding
  90" x 108" batting

You will also need:

  paper-backed fusible web
  thread to match appliqué fabrics

CUTTING OUT THE PIECES

All measurements include a ¼" seam allowance. Follow
Rotary Cutting*, page 144, to cut fabric.*

1. **From white print:** ☐
   - Cut 4 selvage-to-selvage strips 8"w. From these strips, cut a total of 20 **squares** 8" x 8".
   - Cut 1 selvage-to-selvage strip 9½"w. From this strip, cut 4 squares 9½" x 9½" for **border corner squares**.
   - Cut 2 lengthwise strips 9½" x 78½" for **side inner borders**.
   - Cut 2 lengthwise strips 9½" x 63½" for **top/bottom inner borders**.

2. **From mauve print:**
   - Cut 2 lengthwise strips 3" x 99½" for **side outer borders**.
   - Cut 2 lengthwise strips 3" x 81½" for **top/bottom outer borders**.
   - From remaining fabric width, cut 8 strips 6¼"w. From these strips, cut a total of 40 squares 6¼" x 6¼". Cut each square once diagonally to make 80 **triangles**.

square (cut 40)   **triangle** (cut 80)

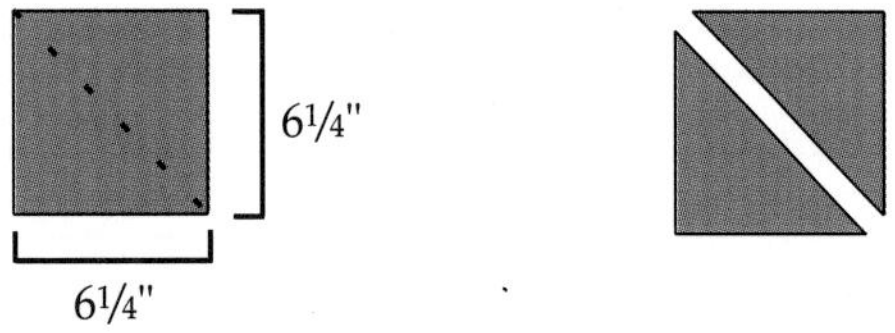

6¼"

6¼"

3. **From mauve/blue floral:**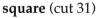
   - Cut 5 selvage-to-selvage strips 6¼"w. From these strips, cut a total of 31 squares 6¼" x 6¼". Cut each square once diagonally to make 62 **triangles**.

square (cut 31)   **triangle** (cut 62)

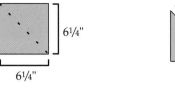

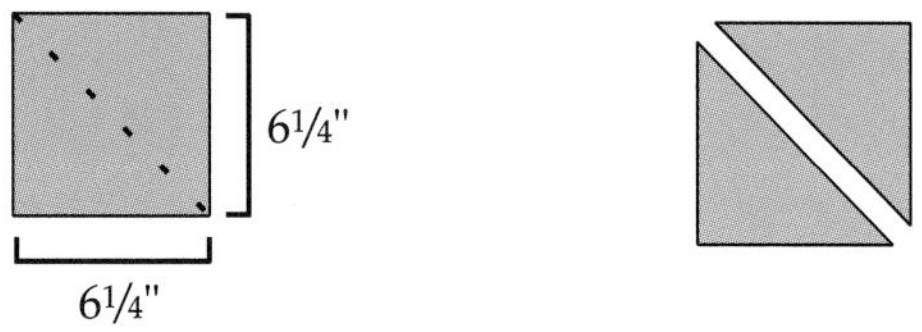

6¼"

6¼"

   - Cut 2 selvage-to-selvage strips 4⅝"w. From these strips, cut a total of 18 squares. Cut each square once diagonally to make 36 **small triangles**.

square (cut 18)   **small triangle** (cut 36)

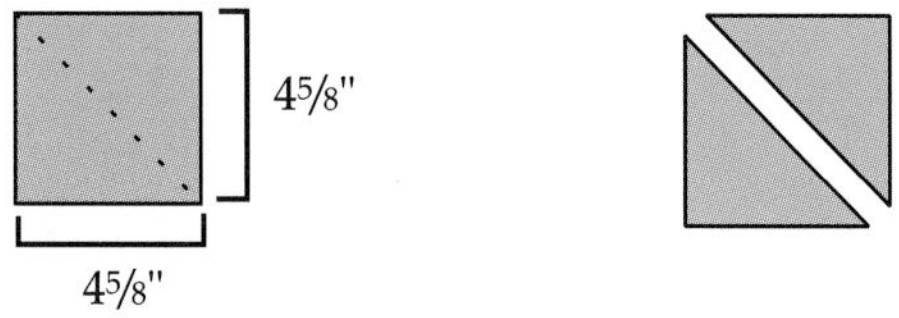

4⅝"

4⅝"

4. **From pink print:** ▨
   - Cut 3 selvage-to-selvage strips 8"w. From these strips, cut a total of 12 **squares** 8" x 8".

5. **From light blue print:** ▨
   - Cut 3 selvage-to-selvage strips 4¼"w. From these strips, cut a total of 14 **rectangles** 4¼" x 8".
   - Cut 4 **squares** 4¼" x 4¼".

CUTTING OUT THE APPLIQUÉS

*Follow **Preparing Appliqué Pieces**, page 148, to cut pieces using **Appliqué Patterns**, pages 139 - 141.*

1. **From mauve/blue floral:** ▨
   - Cut 32 **medium flowers**.

2. **From pink print:** ▨
   - Cut 32 **medium flowers**.
   - Cut 8 **small flowers**.
   - Cut 22 **small flower centers**.

3. **From light blue print:** ▨
   - Cut 18 **swags**.
   - Cut 2 **corner swags**.
   - Cut 76 **bow inner loops**.
   - Cut 2 **streamers** (1 in reverse).

4. **From blue:** ▨
   - Cut 18 **swags**.
   - Cut 2 **corner swags**.
   - Cut 38 **bows**.
   - Cut 2 **streamers** (1 in reverse).

5. **From green:**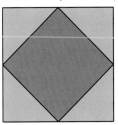
   - Cut 92 **leaves** (46 in reverse).
   - Cut 40 pieces ³⁄₈" x 6" for **short stems**.
   - Cut 20 pieces ³⁄₈" x 7¹⁄₂" for **long stems**.
6. **From mauve:**
   - Cut 22 **large flowers**.
   - Cut 12 **medium flowers**.
7. **From dark mauve print:**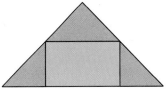
   - Cut 22 **small flowers**.
   - Cut 76 **large flower centers**.
   - Cut 8 **small flower centers**.

ASSEMBLING THE QUILT TOP

Follow Piecing and Pressing, page 146, to make quilt top.

1. Assemble 1 **square** and 4 **triangles** as shown to make **Block A**. Make 12 **Block A's**.

Block A (make 12)

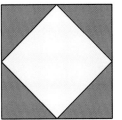

2. Assemble 1 **square** and 4 **triangles** as shown to make **Block B**. Make 20 **Block B's**.

Block B (make 20)

3. Follow **Satin Stitch Appliqué**, page 148, and **Quilt Top Diagram**, page 137, to appliqué **flowers**, **leaves**, **stems**, and **bows** to **Block B's**.

4. Assemble 1 **rectangle**, 2 **small triangles**, and 1 **triangle** as shown to make **Side Setting Triangle**. Make 14 **Side Setting Triangles**.

Side Setting Triangle (make 14)

5. Assemble 1 **square** and 2 **small triangles** as shown to make **Corner Setting Triangle**. Make 4 **Corner Setting Triangles**.

Corner Setting Triangle (make 4)

6. Referring to **Assembly Diagram**, page 136, assemble **Block A's**, **Block B's**, **Side Setting Triangles**, and **Corner Setting Triangles** into rows; sew rows together to complete center section of quilt top.

7. Refer to Steps 1 and 2 of **Adding Squared Borders**, page 150, to trim **top/bottom** and **side inner borders** to fit raw edges of center section of quilt top.

8. Assemble 2 **border corner squares** and 1 **side inner border** as shown to make **Side Inner Border Unit**. Make 2 **Side Inner Border Units**.

Side Inner Border Unit (make 2)

9. Set aside 4 **small flowers**, 4 **small flower centers**, and 8 **leaves** (4 in reverse), which will be appliquéd over remaining corner seams after border is attached to center section of quilt top. Follow **Satin Stitch Appliqué**, page 148, and **Quilt Top Diagram**, page 137, to appliqué remaining **flowers**, **leaves**, **swags**, **bows**, and **streamers** to **top/bottom inner borders** and **Side Inner Border Units**.

10. Follow **Adding Squared Borders**, page 150, and **Quilt Top Diagram** to attach **top** and **bottom inner borders** and then **Side Inner Border Units** to center section of quilt top. Appliqué pieces set aside in Step 8 over corner border seamlines.

11. Add **top**, **bottom**, and then **side outer borders** to complete **Quilt Top**.

COMPLETING THE QUILT

1. Follow **Quilting**, page 151, **Quilting Diagram**, and **Serpentine Quilting Pattern**, page 141, to mark, layer, and quilt.

2. Cut a 36" square of binding fabric. Follow **Making Continuous Bias Strip Binding**, page 155, to make approximately 11 yds of 2¹⁄₂"w bias binding.

3. Follow **Attaching Binding with Mitered Corners**, page 155, to attach binding to quilt.

Quilting Diagram

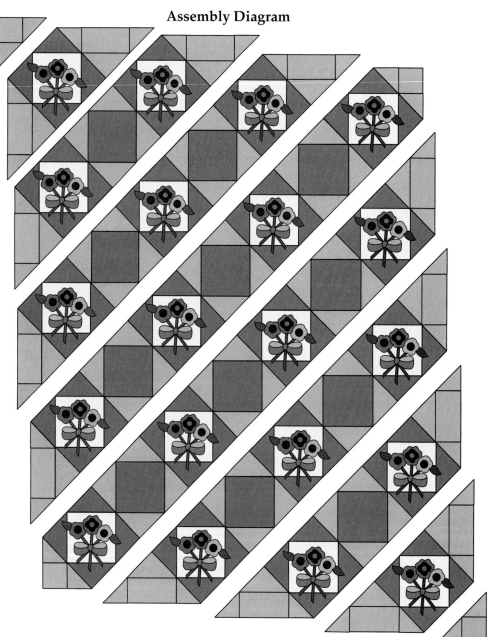

Assembly Diagram

136

NOSEGAY NIGHTGOWN

SUPPLIES

    a cotton nightgown
    scraps of pink and green fabrics for appliqué
    1"w pregathered lace trim with insertion
      header
    1/4"w ribbon
    decorative buttons
    paper-backed fusible web
    embroidery floss to match scrap fabrics and
      buttons

MAKING THE NIGHTGOWN

1. Wash, dry, and press nightgown, fabrics, lace trim, and ribbon.
2. Measure around neck edge and add 1". Cut lace trim the determined measurement. Press ends of lace trim 1/2" to wrong side. Place lace trim along neck edge on right side of nightgown. Topstitch lace trim in place. Repeat for each sleeve edge.
3. Use **Nightgown Flower** and **Nightgown Leaf Patterns** and follow **Preparing Appliqué Pieces**, page 148, to cut desired number of appliqué pieces. Referring to photo, fuse appliqués to nightgown.
4. Use 3 strands of floss to work **Blanket Stitch**, page 158, around edges of appliqués; work **Stem Stitch**, page 158, for stems.
5. Sew 1 button to center of each flower with matching floss. If desired, replace buttons on nightgown with decorative buttons.
6. Tie ribbon into a bow. Use a small safety pin on inside of nightgown to attach bow to front over flower stems.

Nightgown Flower Pattern

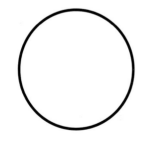

Nightgown Leaf Pattern

ROSY TABLE TOPPER

TABLE TOPPER SIZE: 45" x 45"

YARDAGE REQUIREMENTS

Yardage is based on 45"w fabric.

☐ 44" x 44" square of white print for table topper

◩ 1 fat quarter (18" x 22" piece) **each** of mauve/blue floral, pink print, dark mauve print, mauve, light blue print, blue, and green for appliqués
  5 yds of 2 1/2"w bias binding (pieced if necessary)

You will also need:
  paper-backed fusible web
  thread to match appliqué fabrics

CUTTING OUT THE APPLIQUÉS

*Follow **Preparing Appliqué Pieces**, page 148, to cut pieces using **Appliqué Patterns**, pages 139 - 141.*

1. **From mauve/blue floral:**
   - Cut 4 **medium flowers**.
2. **From pink print:**
   - Cut 4 **medium flowers**.
   - Cut 4 **small flower centers**.
3. **From dark mauve print:**
   - Cut 4 **small flowers**.
   - Cut 8 **large flower centers**.
4. **From mauve:**
   - Cut 4 **large flowers**.
5. **From light blue print:**
   - Cut 8 **bow inner loops**.
6. **From blue:**
   - Cut 4 **bows**.
7. **From green:**
   - Cut 8 **leaves** (4 in reverse).
   - Cut 8 pieces 3/8" x 6" for **short stems**.
   - Cut 4 pieces 3/8" x 7 1/2" for **long stems**.

MAKING THE TABLE TOPPER

1. Referring to photo, follow **Satin Stitch Appliqué**, page 148, to appliqué **flowers**, **leaves**, **stems**, and **bow** to each corner of table topper.
2. Follow **Attaching Binding with Mitered Corners**, page 155, to attach binding to table topper.

PILLOW SHAMS

PILLOW SHAM SIZE: 20" x 26"

YARDAGE REQUIREMENTS

Yardage is based on 45"w fabric.

☐ 3 yds of white print

▨ ¼ yd of mauve for binding

▧ scraps of pink print, mauve/blue floral, light blue print, blue, dark mauve print, mauve, and green for appliqués

You will also need:
paper-backed fusible web
thread to match appliqué fabrics

CUTTING OUT THE PIECES

1. **From white print:** ☐
   - Cut 1 square 18" x 18". Cut once diagonally to cut 2 triangles for **flaps**.
   - Cut 2 rectangles 21" x 27" for **sham tops**.
   - Cut 4 rectangles 16½" x 21" for **sham backs**.

2. **From mauve:** ▨
   - Cut 2 selvage-to-selvage **strips** 2½"w for binding.

CUTTING OUT THE APPLIQUÉS

*Follow **Preparing Appliqué Pieces**, page 148, to cut pieces using **Appliqué Patterns**, pages 139 - 141.*

1. **From pink print:** ▨
   - Cut 2 **medium flowers**.
   - Cut 2 **small flower centers**.

2. **From mauve/blue floral:** ▨
   - Cut 2 **medium flowers**.

3. **From light blue print:** ▨
   - Cut 4 **bow inner loops**.

4. **From blue:** ▨
   - Cut 2 **bows**.

5. **From dark mauve print:** ▨
   - Cut 2 **small flowers**.
   - Cut 4 **large flower centers**.

6. **From mauve:** ▨
   - Cut 2 **large flowers**.

7. **From green:** ▨
   - Cut 4 **leaves** (2 in reverse).
   - Cut 4 pieces ³/₈" x 6" for **short stems**.
   - Cut 2 pieces ³/₈" x 7½" for **long stems**.

MAKING THE SHAMS

1. Referring to photo, follow **Satin Stitch Appliqué**, page 148, to appliqué **flowers**, **stems**, **leaves**, and **bow** to each **flap**.

2. Referring to Steps 3 - 6 and 8 of **Attaching Binding with Mitered Corners**, page 155, use 2½"w **strips** to bind lower edges of each flap. Trim binding even with edge of flap at each end.

3. On each sham back piece, press one 21" edge ½" to wrong side; press ½" to wrong side again and stitch in place.

4. For each **sham back**, place 2 sham back pieces right side up. Referring to **Fig. 1**, overlap finished edges and baste in place.

Fig. 1

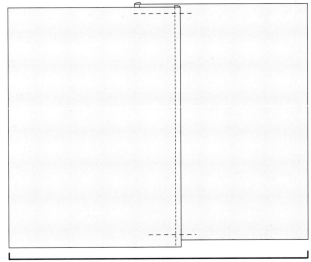

27"

5. To complete each sham, match right sides and long raw edges and center flap on sham back. Place **sham top**, wrong side up, on flap and back. Stitch through all layers ½" from raw edges. Cut corners diagonally; remove basting threads at opening. Turn sham right side out; press.

Small Flower Pattern

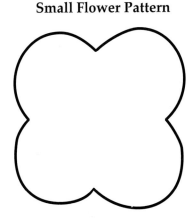

139

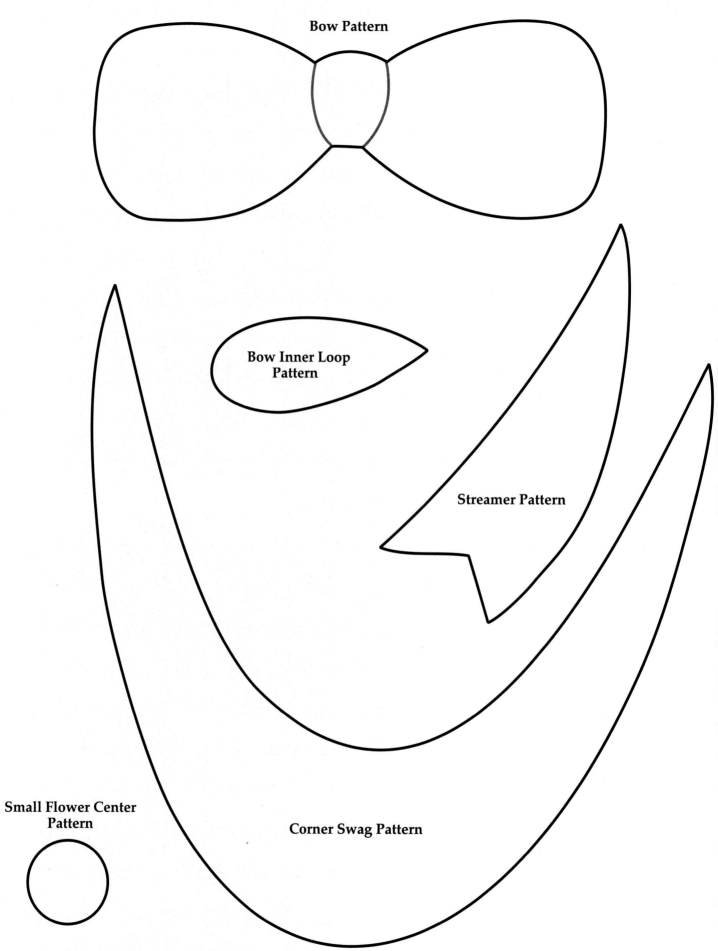

Bow Pattern

Bow Inner Loop Pattern

Streamer Pattern

Small Flower Center Pattern

Corner Swag Pattern

140

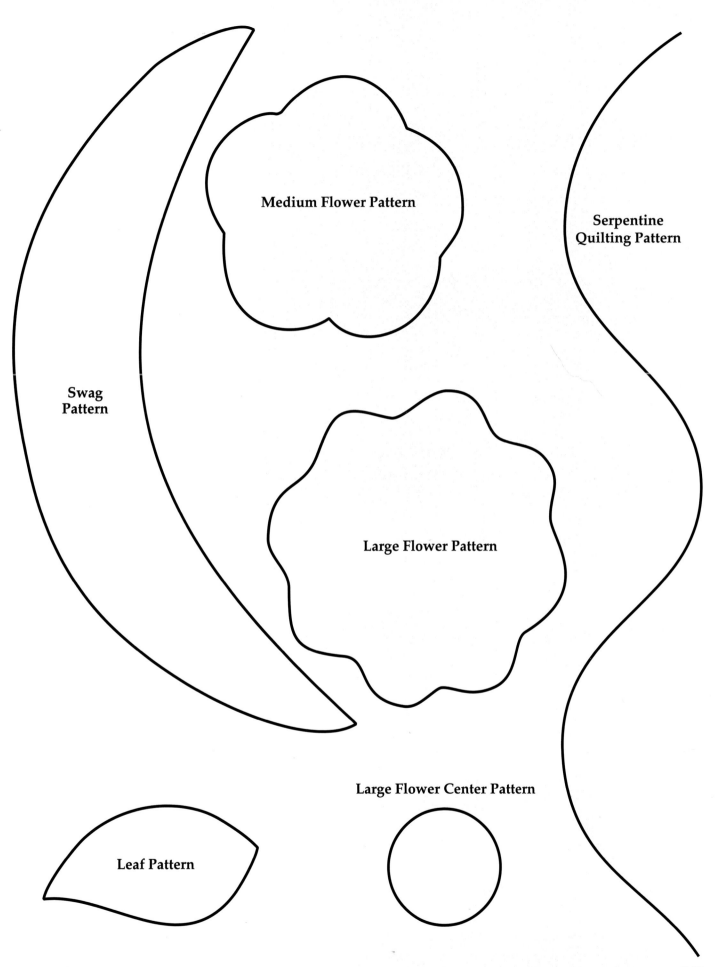

Medium Flower Pattern

Serpentine
Quilting Pattern

Swag
Pattern

Large Flower Pattern

Large Flower Center Pattern

Leaf Pattern

141

GENERAL INSTRUCTIONS

Complete instructions are given for making each of the quilts and other projects shown in this book. Skill levels are included for quilts and wall hangings. Before beginning a project, we encourage you to carefully read all of these general instructions, study the color photographs, and familiarize yourself with the individual project instructions.

BASIC QUILTING SUPPLIES

This list includes the supplies needed for basic quick-method quiltmaking. Unless otherwise specified, all items may be found in your favorite fabric store or quilt shop.

Batting — Batting is most commonly available in polyester, cotton, or a polyester/cotton blend. Beginning quilters may want to choose a low-loft polyester bonded batting since it is thinner and easier to quilt. Bonded batting has been through a process to help prevent the fibers from separating.

Cutting mat — A cutting mat is a special mat designed to be used with a rotary cutter. A mat that measures approximately 18" x 24" is a good size for most cutting.

Eraser — A soft white fabric eraser or white art eraser may be used to remove pencil marks from fabric. Do not use a colored eraser, as the dye may discolor fabric.

Iron — An iron with both steam and dry settings and a smooth, clean soleplate is necessary for proper pressing.

Marking tools — There are many different types of marking tools available (see **Marking Quilting Lines**, page 151). A silver quilter's pencil is a good marker for both light and dark fabrics. You will probably want to experiment with different markers to decide which types you prefer for different applications.

Needles — Two types of needles are used for hand sewing, betweens and sharps. *Betweens*, used for quilting, are short and strong for stitching through layered fabric and batting. Beginning quilters may wish to try a size 8 or 9 needle. *Sharps* are longer, thinner needles used for basting and other hand sewing. For *sewing machine needles*, we recommend size 10 to 14 or 70 to 90 universal (sharp-pointed) needles made for woven fabrics. For tying quilts, you will need a large *darning* needle.

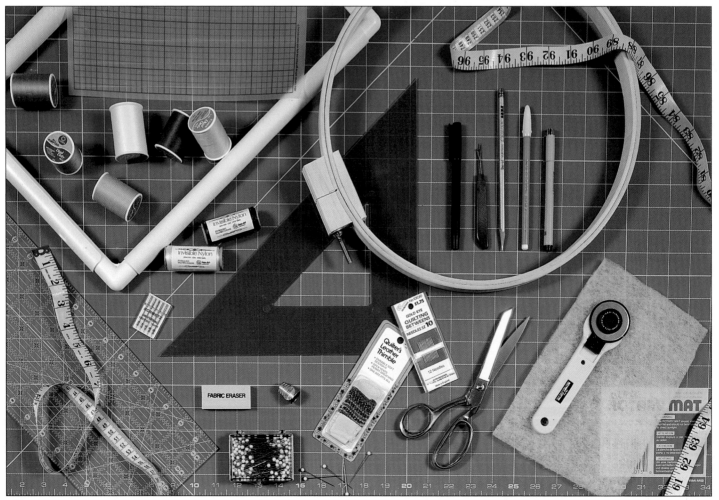

Permanent fine-point marker — A permanent marker is used to mark templates and stencils and to sign and date quilts. Test marker on fabric to make sure it will not bleed or wash out.

Pins — Straight pins made especially for quilting are extra long with large, round heads. Some quilters prefer extra-fine dressmaker's silk pins.

Quilting hoop or frame — Quilting hoops and frames are designed to securely hold the 3 layers of a quilt together while you quilt. Many different types and sizes are available, including round and oval wooden hoops, frames made of rigid plastic pipe, and large floor frames made of either material. A 14" or 16" hoop allows you to quilt in your lap and makes your quilting portable.

Rotary cutter — The rotary cutter is the essential tool for quick-method quilting techniques. The cutter consists of a round, sharp blade mounted on a handle with a retractable blade guard for safety. It should be used only with a cutting mat and rotary cutting ruler. Two sizes are generally available; we recommend the larger size.

Rotary cutting rulers — A rotary cutting ruler is a thick, clear plastic ruler made specifically for use with a rotary cutter. It should have accurate 1/8" crosswise and lengthwise markings and markings for 45° and 60° angles. A 6" x 24" ruler is a good size for most cutting. An additional 6" x 12" ruler or 12½" square ruler is helpful when cutting wider pieces.

Scissors — Although most cutting will be done with a rotary cutter, sharp, high-quality scissors are still needed for some cutting. A separate pair of scissors for cutting paper and plastic is recommended. Smaller scissors are handy for clipping threads.

Seam ripper — A good seam ripper with a fine point is useful for ripping out stitching mistakes.

Sewing machine — A sewing machine that produces a good, even straight stitch is all that is necessary for most quilting. Clean and oil your machine often and keep the tension set properly. Zigzag stitch capability is necessary for machine appliqué.

Tape measure — A flexible 120" long tape measure is helpful for measuring a quilt top before adding borders.

Template material — Sheets of translucent plastic, often pre-marked with a grid, are made especially for making quilting templates and stencils.

Thimble — Thimbles are available in metal, plastic, or leather and in many sizes and styles. Choose a thimble that fits well and is comfortable.

Thread — Several types of thread are used for quiltmaking. *General-purpose* sewing thread is used for basting, piecing, and some appliquéing. Buy high-quality cotton or cotton-covered polyester thread in light and dark neutrals, such as ecru and grey, for your basic supplies. *Quilting* thread is stronger than regular sewing thread, and some brands have a coating to make them slide more easily through the quilt layers. Some machine appliqué projects in this book use *transparent monofilament* (clear nylon) thread. Use a very fine, soft nylon thread that is not stiff or wiry. Choose clear nylon thread for white or light fabrics or smoke nylon thread for darker fabrics.

Triangle — A large plastic right-angle triangle (available in art and office supply stores) is useful in rotary cutting for making first cuts to "square up" raw edges and for checking to see that cuts remain at right angles to fold.

FABRICS

SELECTING FABRICS

The yardage requirements listed for each project are based on 45" wide fabric with a "usable" width of 42" to allow for shrinkage and trimming selvages. The required length of each fabric also takes into account that fabric may not have been cut perfectly straight when cut from the bolt.

The colors you choose for your quilt are important. Color is seen first, even before design and workmanship. Light colors emphasize an area of a quilt, while dark colors cause an area to recede. Contrasting colors will give your quilt movement and sparkle.

Choose high-quality medium-weight 100% cotton fabrics such as broadcloth or calico. All-cotton fabrics hold a crease better, fray less, and are easier to quilt than cotton/polyester blends. All the fabrics for a quilt should be of comparable weight and weave. Check the end of the fabric bolt for fiber content and width.

PREPARING FABRICS

All fabrics should be washed, dried, and pressed before cutting.

1. To check colorfastness before washing, cut a small piece of the fabric and place in a glass of hot water with a little detergent. Leave fabric in water for a few minutes. Remove from water and blot fabric with white paper towels. If any color bleeds onto the towels, wash the fabric separately with warm water and detergent, then rinse until the water runs clear. If fabric continues to bleed, choose another fabric.

2. Unfold yardage and separate fabrics by color. To help reduce raveling, use scissors to snip off small corners of fabric pieces (**Fig. 1**). Machine wash in warm water with a small amount of mild laundry detergent. Do not use fabric softener. Rinse well and then dry fabrics in the dryer, checking long fabric lengths occasionally to make sure they are not tangling.

Fig. 1

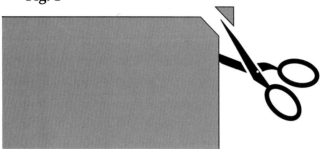

3. To make ironing easier, remove fabrics from dryer while they are slightly damp. Refold each fabric lengthwise (as it was on the bolt) with wrong sides together and matching selvages. If necessary, adjust slightly at selvages so that fold lies flat. Press each fabric with a steam iron set on "Cotton".

ROTARY CUTTING

*Based on the idea that you can easily cut strips of fabric and then cut those strips into smaller pieces, rotary cutting has brought speed and accuracy to quiltmaking. Observe safety precautions when using the rotary cutter since it is extremely sharp. Develop a habit of retracting the blade guard **just before** making a cut and closing it **immediately afterward** before laying down the cutter.*

1. Follow **Preparing Fabrics**, page 143, to wash, dry, and press fabrics. Fabrics should be pressed in half lengthwise with wrong sides together.

2. Most strips are cut from the selvage-to-selvage width of a length of fabric. Place fabric on the cutting mat as shown in **Fig. 2** with the fold of the fabric toward you. To straighten the uneven fabric edge, make the first "squaring up" cut by placing the right edge of the rotary cutting ruler over the left raw edge of the fabric. Place right-angle triangle with the lower edge carefully aligned with the fold and the left edge against the ruler (**Fig. 2**). Hold the ruler firmly with your left hand, placing your little finger off the left edge of the ruler to anchor it. Remove the triangle, pick up the rotary cutter, and retract the blade guard. Using a smooth, downward motion, make the cut by running the blade of the rotary cutter firmly along the right edge of the ruler (**Fig. 3**). **Always** cut in a direction **away** from your body and **immediately** close the blade guard after each cut.

Fig. 2

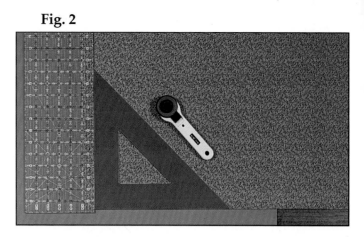

Fig. 3

3. After squaring up, cut the strips required for the project. Place the ruler over the cut edge of the fabric, aligning desired marking on the ruler with the cut edge of the fabric (**Fig. 4**). When cutting several strips from a single piece of fabric, it is important to occasionally use the ruler and triangle to ensure that cuts are still at a perfect right angle to the fold. If not, repeat Step 2 to straighten.

Fig. 4

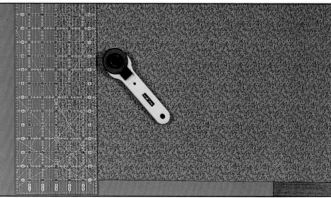

4. To square up selvage ends of a strip before cutting pieces, refer to **Fig. 5** and place folded strip on mat with selvage ends to your right. Aligning a horizontal marking on ruler with 1 long edge of strip, use rotary cutter to trim off selvage to make end of strip square and even (**Fig. 5**). Turn strip (or entire mat) so that cut end is to your left before making subsequent cuts.

Fig. 5

5. Pieces such as rectangles and squares can now be cut from strips. (Cutting other shapes like diamonds is discussed in individual project instructions.) Usually, strips remain folded, and pieces are cut in pairs after ends of strips are squared up. To cut squares or rectangles from a strip, place ruler over left end of strip, aligning desired marking on ruler with cut end of strip. To ensure perfectly square cuts, align a horizontal marking on ruler with 1 long edge of strip (**Fig. 6**). Make cut as in Step 2.

Fig. 6

6. After some practice, you may want to try stacking up to 6 fabric layers when making cuts. When stacking strips, match long cut edges and follow Step 4 to square up ends of strip stack. Carefully turn stack (or entire mat) so that squared-up ends are at your left before making subsequent cuts.

7. When cutting a strip set into smaller units, align a seam in strip set with a horizontal marking on the ruler to maintain square cuts (**Fig. 7**). We do not recommend stacking strip sets for rotary cutting.

Fig. 7

8. Most borders for quilts in this book are cut along the more stable lengthwise grain to minimize wavy edges caused by stretching. To remove selvages before cutting lengthwise strips, place fabric on mat with selvages to your left and squared-up end at bottom of mat. Placing ruler over selvage and using squared-up edge instead of fold, follow Step 2 to cut away selvages as you did raw edges (**Fig. 8**). After making a cut the length of the mat, move the next section to be cut onto the mat. Repeat until you have removed selvages from required length of fabric.

Fig. 8

9. After removing selvages, place ruler over left edge of fabric, aligning desired marking on ruler with cut edge of fabric. Make cuts as in Step 3. After each cut, move next section of fabric onto mat as in Step 8.

PIECING AND PRESSING

Precise cutting, followed by accurate piecing and careful pressing, will ensure that all the pieces of your quilt top will fit together, resulting in a smooth, flat quilt top without wavy edges or misshapen corners.

PIECING

Set sewing machine stitch length for approximately 11 stitches per inch. Use a new, sharp needle suited for medium-weight woven fabric. For good results, it is **essential** that you stitch with an **accurate 1/4" seam allowance**. On many sewing machines, the measurement from the needle to the outer edge of the presser foot is 1/4". If this is the case with your machine, you may use the presser foot as a guide. If not, measure 1/4" from the needle and mark with a piece of masking tape. Designed for quilters, special presser feet that are exactly 1/4" wide are also available for most sewing machines.

Use general-purpose sewing thread (not quilting thread) in the needle and in the bobbin. Stitch first on a scrap of fabric to check upper and bobbin thread tension and make any adjustments necessary.

When piecing, **always** place pieces **right sides together** and **match raw edges**; pin if necessary. (If using straight pins while piecing, remove the pins just before they reach the sewing machine needle.)

Chain Piecing

Chain piecing whenever possible will make your work go much faster and will usually result in more accurate piecing. Stack the pieces you will be sewing beside your machine in the order you will need them and in a position that will allow you to easily pick them up. Pick up each pair of pieces, carefully place them together as they will be sewn and feed them into the machine 1 after the other. Stop between each pair only long enough to pick up the next and don't cut thread between pairs (**Fig. 9**). After all pieces are sewn, cut threads, press, and go on to the next step, chain piecing again whenever possible.

Fig. 9

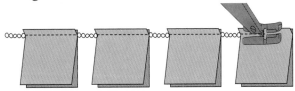

Making Triangle-Squares

The grid method for making triangle-squares is faster and more accurate than cutting and sewing individual triangles. Stitching before cutting the triangle-squares apart also prevents stretching the bias edges.

1. Follow project instructions to cut rectangles or squares of fabric for making triangle-squares. With right sides together and matching raw edges, press the fabrics.

2. On the wrong side of the lighter fabric, mark a grid of squares similar to one shown in **Fig. 10**. The size and number of squares will be given in the project instructions.

Fig. 10

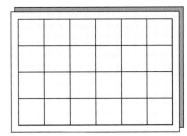

3. Following the example given in the project instructions, draw 1 diagonal line through each square in the grid (**Fig. 11**).

Fig. 11

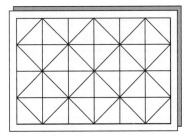

4. Stitch 1/4" on each side of all diagonal lines. In some cases, stitching may be done in a single continuous line. Project instructions include a diagram similar to **Fig. 12** which shows stitching lines and the direction of the stitching.

Fig. 12

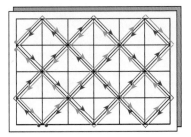

5. Use rotary cutter and ruler to cut along all drawn lines of the grid. Each square of the grid will yield two triangle-squares (**Fig. 13**).

Fig. 13

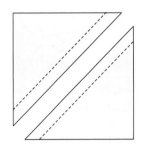

6. Carefully press triangle-squares open, pressing seam allowance toward darker fabric. Trim off points of seam allowances that extend beyond edge of triangle-square (**Fig. 14**).

Fig. 14

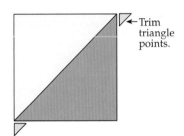

← Trim triangle points.

Sewing Across Seam Intersections

When sewing across the intersection of two seams, place pieces right sides together and match seams, making sure seam allowances are facing opposite directions. To prevent fabric from shifting, you may wish to pin in place (**Fig. 15**).

Fig. 15

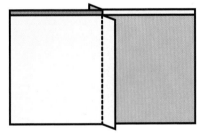

Sewing Bias Seams

Care should be used in handling and stitching bias edges, since they stretch easily. After sewing the seam, carefully press seam allowances to 1 side, making sure not to stretch the fabric.

Working with Diamond Shapes

Piecing diamonds or parallelograms requires special handling. For best results, carefully follow the steps below to assemble the diamond sections of a block.

1. When sewing 2 diamond or parallelogram pieces together, place pieces right sides together, carefully matching edges; pin. Mark a small dot $1/4$" from corner of 1 piece as shown in **Fig. 16**. Stitch pieces together in the direction shown in **Fig. 16**, stopping at center of dot and backstitching.

Fig. 16

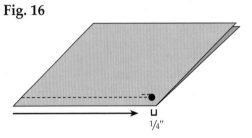

$1/4$"

2. To add the corner squares and side triangles to diamond sections, mark each corner to be set in with a small dot (**Fig. 17**). Match right sides and pin the square or triangle to the diamond on the left. Stitch seam from the outer edge to the dot and backstitch (**Fig. 18**).

Fig. 17

Fig. 18

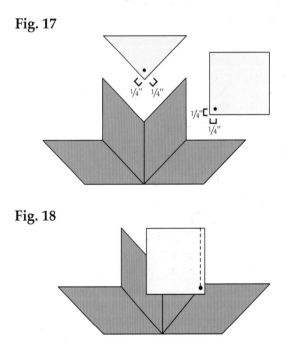

3. To sew the second seam, pivot the added square or triangle to match raw edges of next diamond. Pin and sew as before, beginning with the needle in the hole of the last stitch taken and sewing to the edge of the fabric (**Fig. 19**).

Fig. 19

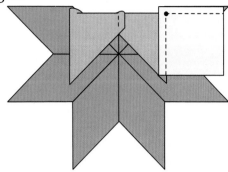

Trimming Seam Allowances

When sewing with diamond or triangle pieces, some seam allowances may extend beyond the edges of the sewn pieces. Trim these "dog ears" even with pieces to which they are joined (**Fig. 20**).

Fig. 20

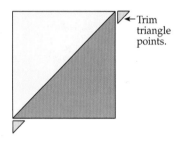

← Trim triangle points.

PRESSING

Use a steam iron set on "Cotton" for all pressing. Press as you sew, taking care to prevent small folds along seamlines. Seam allowances are almost always pressed to 1 side, usually toward the darker fabric. However, to reduce bulk it may occasionally be necessary to press seam allowances toward the lighter fabric or even to press them open. In order to prevent a dark fabric seam allowance from showing through a light fabric, trim the darker seam allowance slightly narrower than the lighter seam allowance.

MACHINE APPLIQUÉ

The projects in this book feature 2 kinds of machine appliqué: **satin stitch appliqué,** *a decorative stitch that uses a different color of thread to match each appliqué fabric, and* **almost invisible appliqué,** *which is an adaptation of satin stitch appliqué that uses clear nylon thread to secure the appliqué pieces. Preparation for both types of appliqué is the same.*

PREPARING APPLIQUÉ PIECES

Patterns are printed in reverse to enable you to use our speedy method of preparing appliqués.

1. Place paper-backed fusible web, web side down, over appliqué pattern. Use a pencil to trace pattern onto paper side of web as many times as indicated in project instructions for a single fabric. Repeat for additional patterns and fabrics.
2. Follow manufacturer's instructions to fuse traced patterns to wrong side of fabrics. Do not remove paper backing.
3. Some projects may have pieces that are given as measurements (such as a 2" x 4" rectangle) instead of drawn patterns. Fuse web to wrong side of fabrics indicated for these pieces.
4. Use scissors to cut out appliqué pieces along traced lines; use rotary cutter and ruler to cut out appliqué pieces given as measurements. Remove paper backing from all pieces.

SATIN STITCH APPLIQUÉ

A good satin stitch is a thick, smooth, almost solid line of zigzag stitching that covers the raw edges of appliqué pieces. Designs with layered appliqué pieces should be stitched beginning with the bottom pieces and ending with the pieces on top.

1. Referring to diagram and/or photo, arrange appliqués on the background fabric and fuse in place.
2. Place a stabilizer, such as paper or any of the commercially available products, on wrong side of background fabric before stitching appliqués in place.
3. Thread needle of sewing machine with general-purpose thread that matches appliqué piece. Use thread that matches the background fabric in the bobbin for all stitching. Set sewing machine for a medium width zigzag stitch (approximately 1/8") and a very short stitch length. Set upper tension slightly looser than for regular stitching.

4. Beginning on as straight an edge as possible, position fabric so that most of the satin stitch will be on the appliqué piece. Do not backstitch; hold upper thread toward you and sew over it 2 - 3 stitches to anchor thread. Following Steps 5 - 8 for stitching corners and curves, stitch over exposed raw edges of appliqué pieces, changing thread color as necessary.

5. (*Note: Dots on **Figs. 21 - 26** indicate where to leave needle in fabric when pivoting.*) For **outside corners**, stitch ⅛" past the corner, stopping with the needle in **background** fabric (**Fig. 21**). Raise presser foot. Pivot project, lower presser foot, and stitch adjacent side (**Fig. 22**).

Fig. 21 **Fig. 22**

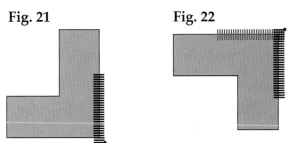

6. For **inside corners**, stitch ⅛" past the corner, stopping with the needle in **appliqué** fabric (**Fig. 23**). Raise presser foot. Pivot project, lower presser foot, and stitch adjacent side (**Fig. 24**).

Fig. 23 **Fig. 24**

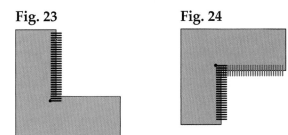

7. When stitching **outside** curves, stop with needle in **background** fabric. Raise presser foot and pivot project as needed. Lower presser foot and continue stitching, pivoting as often as necessary to follow curve (**Fig. 25**).

Fig. 25

8. When stitching **inside** curves, stop with needle in **appliqué** fabric. Raise presser foot and pivot project as needed. Lower presser foot and continue stitching, pivoting as often as necessary to follow curve (**Fig. 26**).

Fig. 26

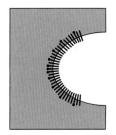

9. Do not backstitch at end of stitching. Pull threads to wrong side of background fabric; knot thread and trim ends. Remove paper or stabilizer.

ALMOST INVISIBLE APPLIQUÉ
Transparent monofilament (clear nylon) thread is available in 2 colors: clear and smoke. Use clear on white or very light fabrics and smoke on darker colors.

1. Referring to diagram and/or photo, arrange appliqués on the background fabric and fuse in place.
2. Place a stabilizer, such as paper or any of the commercially available products, on wrong side of background fabric before stitching appliqués in place.
3. Thread sewing machine with transparent monofilament thread; use general-purpose thread that matches background fabric in bobbin.
4. Set sewing machine for a very narrow (approximately ¹⁄₁₆") zigzag stitch and a short stitch length. You may find that loosening the top tension slightly will yield a smoother stitch.
5. Begin by stitching 2 or 3 stitches in place (drop feed dogs or set stitch length at 0) to anchor thread. Most of the zigzag stitch should be done on the appliqué with the right edge of the stitch falling at the very outside edge of the appliqué (**Fig. 27**). Follow Steps 5 - 8 of **Satin Stitch Appliqué** for stitching corners and curves, stitching over all exposed raw edges of appliqué pieces.

Fig. 27

6. End stitching by sewing 2 or 3 stitches in place to anchor thread. Trim thread ends close to fabric.

BORDERS

Borders cut along the lengthwise grain will lay flatter and smoother than borders cut along the crosswise grain. Lengthwise-grain borders are especially important for bed-size quilts, since the more stable lengthwise grain is less likely to stretch out of shape and cause wavy or "lettuce" edges. Our instructions for cutting borders for bed-size quilts also include an extra 2" at each end for "insurance"; borders will be trimmed after measuring completed center section of quilt top. And, as always, you should match right sides and raw edges and use a 1/4" seam allowance when sewing.

ADDING SQUARED BORDERS

1. Mark the center of each edge of quilt top (**Fig. 28**).

Fig. 28

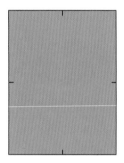

2. Squared borders are usually added to top and bottom, then side edges, of the center section of a quilt top. To add top border, measure across center of quilt top to determine length of border (**Fig. 29**). Trim border to the determined length.

Fig. 29

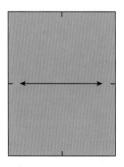

3. Mark center of 1 long edge of border. Matching center marks and raw edges, pin border to quilt top, easing in any fullness; stitch.
4. Repeat Steps 2 and 3 to add bottom border to quilt top.

5. Measure center of quilt top (including attached borders) to determine length of side borders. Repeat Steps 2 and 3 to add side borders to quilt top (**Fig. 30**).

Fig. 30

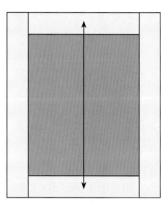

ADDING MITERED BORDERS

1. Mark the center of each edge of quilt top (see **Fig. 28**).
2. Mark center of 1 long edge of top border. Measure across center of quilt top (see **Fig. 29**). Matching center marks and raw edges, pin border to center of quilt top edge. From center of border, measure out 1/2 the width of the quilt top in both directions and mark. Match marks on border with corners of quilt top and pin. Easing in any fullness, pin border to quilt top between center and corners. Sew border to quilt top, beginning and ending seams **exactly** 1/4" from each corner of quilt top and backstitching at beginning and end of stitching (**Fig. 31**).

Fig. 31

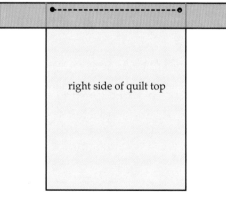

right side of quilt top

3. Repeat Step 2 to sew bottom, then side borders, to center section of quilt top. To temporarily move first 2 borders out of the way, fold and pin ends as shown in **Fig. 32**.

Fig. 32

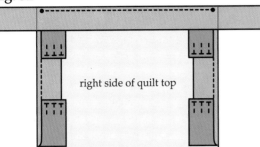

4. Fold 1 corner of quilt top diagonally with right sides together; use rotary cutting ruler to mark stitching line as shown in **Fig. 33**. Pin strips together along drawn line. Sew on drawn line, backstitching at beginning and end of stitching (**Fig. 34**).

Fig. 33   **Fig. 34**

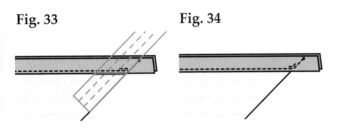

5. Turn mitered corner right side up. Check to see that there is not a gap at the inner end of the seam and that corner does not pucker.
6. Trim seam allowances to 1/4"; press to 1 side.
7. Repeat Steps 4 - 6 to miter each remaining corner.

QUILTING

Quilting holds the 3 layers (top, batting, and backing) of the quilt together. Because marking, layering, and quilting are interrelated and may be done in different orders depending on circumstances, please read this entire section, pages 151 - 154, before beginning the quilting process on your project.

MARKING QUILTING LINES

Lead, silver, and white fabric marking pencils; various types of chalk markers; and fabric marking pens with inks that disappear with exposure to air or water are readily available and work well for different applications. Lead pencils work well on light-colored fabric, but marks may be difficult to remove. White pencils work well on dark-colored fabric, and silver pencils show up well on many colors. Keep pencils sharp to ensure accuracy.

Press down only as hard as necessary to make a visible line. Marks need to remain on the fabric until you are finished quilting, but should be relatively easy to remove after stitching is complete.

When you choose to mark your quilt, whether before or after the layers are basted together, is also a factor in deciding which marking tool to use. If you mark with chalk or a chalk pencil, handling the quilt during basting may rub off the markings. Intricate or ornamental designs may not be practical to mark as you quilt; mark these designs before basting using a more durable marker.

To choose marking tools, take all these factors into consideration and **test** different markers **on scrap fabric** until you find the one that gives the desired result.

TYPES OF QUILTING

In the Ditch

Quilting very close to a seamline (**Fig. 35**) or appliqué (**Fig. 36**) is called "in the ditch" quilting. This type of quilting does not need to be marked and is indicated on our quilting diagrams with blue lines close to seamlines. When quilting in the ditch, quilt on the side **opposite** the seam allowance.

Fig. 35

Fig. 36

Outline Quilting

Quilting approximately ¼" from a seam or appliqué is called "outline" quilting (**Fig. 37**). This type of quilting is indicated on our quilting diagrams by blue lines a short distance from seamlines. Outline quilting may be marked, or you may place ¼"w masking tape along seamlines and quilt along the opposite edge of the tape. (Do not leave tape on quilt longer than necessary, since it may leave an adhesive residue.)

Fig. 37

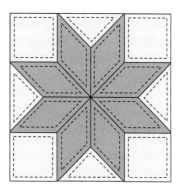

Ornamental Quilting

Quilting decorative lines or designs is called "ornamental" quilting (**Fig. 38**). Ornamental quilting is indicated on our quilting diagrams by blue lines. This type of quilting should be marked before you baste quilt layers together.

Fig. 38

USING QUILTING STENCILS AND TEMPLATES

If your quilt top is light-colored, you may trace the quilting pattern directly onto the quilt top. If your quilt top is dark-colored, you may purchase a quilting stencil or make your own.

1. To make a stencil from a pattern, center template plastic over pattern and use a permanent marker to trace pattern onto plastic. Use a craft knife to cut narrow slits along traced lines (**Fig. 39**).

Fig. 39

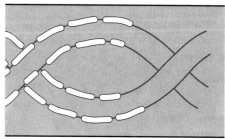

2. To make stencils from a half pattern, draw a line down the center of a sheet of template plastic. Match center of quilting pattern to intersection of drawn line on plastic. Trace half pattern onto plastic. Turn template over and trace pattern again to complete.

3. To draw a pattern for feather designs, cut a piece of paper the size of the border (or other area of your quilt) to be marked. Refer to the project quilting diagram to draw center placement line on paper. Trace feather template pattern included in project instructions onto template plastic and cut out. Placing narrow point of template along placement line, use a pencil to draw feathers, reversing template and adjusting spacing of feathers as necessary on curves and corners (**Figs. 40** and **41**). After pattern is drawn, trace the paper pattern to mark a light-colored quilt top or follow Step 1 to make a stencil for marking a dark-colored quilt top.

Fig. 40

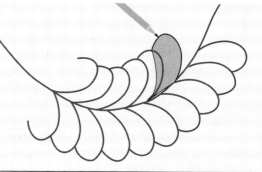

Fig. 41

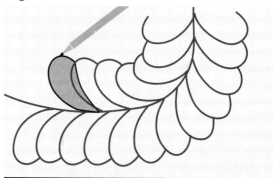

PREPARING BACKING AND BATTING

The backing and batting for a bed-size quilt should be approximately 4" larger on all sides than the quilt top to allow for the quilt top shifting slightly during quilting. Piecing the backing will probably be necessary. For a wall hanging, the backing and batting should be approximately 2" larger on all sides.

1. Measure length and width of quilt top; add 8" (4" for a wall hanging) to each measurement.
2. Cut backing fabric into 2 (or 3, if quilt is wider than 76") lengths slightly longer than the determined measurement. Trim selvages.
3. If using 2 lengths, place lengths with right sides facing and sew long edges together, forming a tube (**Fig. 42**). Match seams and press along 1 fold (**Fig. 43**). Cut along pressed fold to form a single piece (**Fig. 44**).

Fig. 42   **Fig. 43**

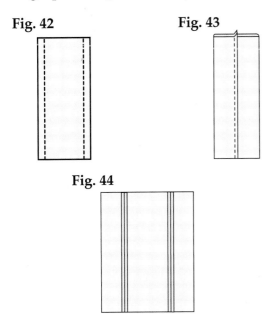

Fig. 44

4. If using 3 lengths, sew long edges together to form a single piece.
5. Trim to correct size, if necessary, and press seam allowances open.
6. Trim batting to same size as backing.

LAYERING THE QUILT

1. Examine wrong side of quilt top closely and trim any seam allowances and clip any threads that may show through the front of the quilt. Press quilt top.
2. If top is to be marked before layering, mark quilting lines on quilt top (see **Marking Quilting Lines**, page 151).

3. Place backing **wrong** side up on a flat surface. Use masking tape to tape backing to surface. Place batting on wrong side of backing fabric. Smooth batting gently, being careful not to stretch or tear. Center quilt top **right** side up on batting. Beginning in the center and working toward outer edges, baste all layers together using long stitches and placing basting lines approximately 4" apart (**Fig. 45**). Smooth fullness or wrinkles toward outer edges.

Fig. 45

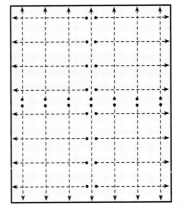

THE QUILTING STITCH

The quilting stitch is a basic running stitch that forms a broken line on the quilt top and backing. Stitches on the quilt top and backing should be straight and equal in length.

1. Secure center of quilt in hoop or frame. Check quilt top and backing to make sure they are smooth. To help prevent puckers, always begin quilting in the center of the quilt and work toward the outside edges.
2. Thread needle with an 18" - 20" length of quilting thread; knot 1 end. Using a thimble, insert needle into quilt top and batting approximately ½" from where you wish to begin quilting. Bring needle up at the point where you wish to begin (**Fig. 46**); when knot catches on quilt top, give thread a quick, short pull to "pop" knot through fabric into batting (**Fig. 47**).

Fig. 46   **Fig. 47**

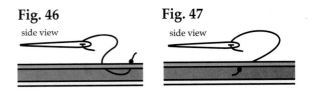

side view   side view

153

3. Holding the needle with your sewing hand and placing your other hand underneath the quilt, use thimble to push the tip of the needle down through all layers. As soon as needle touches your finger underneath, use that finger to push only the tip of the needle back up through the layers to top of quilt. (The amount of the needle showing above the fabric determines the length of the quilting stitch.) Referring to **Fig. 48**, rock the needle up and down, taking 3 - 6 stitches before bringing the needle and thread completely through the layers. Check the back of the quilt to make sure stitches are going through all layers. If you are quilting through a seam allowance or quilting a curve or corner, you may need to take 1 stitch at a time.

Fig. 48

4. When you reach the end of your thread, knot thread close to the fabric and "pop" knot into batting; clip thread close to fabric. Try to keep stitches straight and even; with practice, stitches will become smaller.
5. Stop and move your hoop as often as necessary. You do not have to tie a knot every time you move your hoop; you may leave the thread dangling and pick it up again when you return to that part of the quilt.
6. When you have finished quilting, remove all basting threads. Using a narrow zigzag stitch with a medium stitch length, machine stitch along all edges of quilt top through all layers. Trim batting and backing a scant ¹/₂" larger than quilt top (**Fig. 49**).

Fig. 49

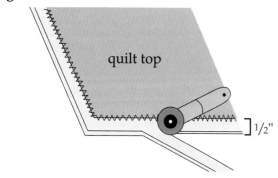

quilt top

¹/₂"

TYING A QUILT

Tied quilts use yarn or floss ties instead of quilting stitches to secure the layers. For a tied quilt, be sure to use bonded batting to prevent separation or bunching when the quilt is laundered. You may also use a higher loft batting than when quilting.

1. Determine where ties will be placed and mark if necessary. Space ties evenly. On a pieced top, tie at corners of blocks or pieces within blocks.
2. Follow **Preparing Backing and Batting**, page 153, and **Layering the Quilt**, page 153, to prepare quilt for tying.
3. Thread a large darning needle with a long length of embroidery floss, yarn, or pearl cotton; do not knot.
4. At each mark or tie location, take a small stitch through all layers of quilt. Pull up floss, but do not cut between stitches (**Fig. 50**). Begin at center of quilt and work toward outside edges, rethreading needle as necessary.

Fig. 50

5. Cut floss between stitches. At each stitch, use a square knot to tie floss securely (**Fig. 51**); trim ties to desired length.

Fig. 51

BINDING

MAKING CONTINUOUS BIAS STRIP BINDING

1. Cut a square from binding fabric the size indicated in the project. Fold square in half diagonally; cut on fold to make 2 triangles.
2. With right sides together and using a ¹/₄" seam allowance, sew triangles together (**Fig. 52**); press seam allowance open.

Fig. 52

3. On wrong side of fabric, draw lines the width specified in the project instructions, usually 2¹/₂" (**Fig. 53**). Cut off any remaining fabric less than this width.

Fig. 53

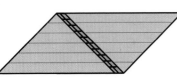

4. With right sides inside, bring short edges together to form a tube (**Fig. 54**).

Fig. 54

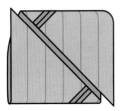

5. Match raw edges so that first drawn line of top section meets second drawn line of bottom section. Insert pins through drawn lines at the point where drawn lines intersect, making sure the pins go through intersections on both sides (**Fig. 55**). Carefully pin edges together. Using a ¹/₄" seam allowance, sew edges together. Press seam allowance open.

Fig. 55

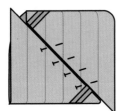

6. To cut continuous strip, begin cutting along first drawn line (**Fig. 56**). Continue cutting along drawn line around tube.

Fig. 56

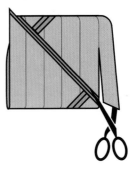

7. Trim each end of bias strip as shown in **Fig. 57**.

Fig. 57

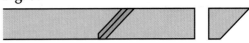

8. Matching wrong sides and raw edges, press binding in half lengthwise.

MAKING STRAIGHT-GRAIN BINDING

usually 2¹/₂" wide

Binding may also be cut from the straight lengthwise or crosswise grain of the fabric. You will find that straight-grain binding works well for small projects and projects with straight edges.

1. Measure each edge of quilt; add 3" to each measurement. Cut lengthwise or crosswise strips of binding fabric the width called for in the project instructions. Strips may be pieced to achieve the necessary length.
2. Matching wrong sides and raw edges, press binding in half lengthwise.

ATTACHING BINDING WITH MITERED CORNERS

*If you wish to attach a hanging sleeve to your quilt or wall hanging, follow **Making a Hanging Sleeve**, page 157, before attaching binding.*

1. Press 1 end of binding diagonally (**Fig. 58**).

Fig. 58

155

2. Matching raw edges of binding to raw edge of quilt top and beginning with pressed end several inches from a corner, pin binding to right side of quilt along 1 side. Lay binding around quilt to make sure that seams in binding will not end up at a corner. Adjust placement if necessary.

3. When you reach the first corner, mark ¹/₄" from corner of quilt (**Fig. 59**).

Fig. 59

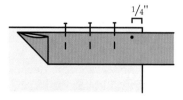

4. Using a ¹/₄" seam allowance, sew binding to quilt, backstitching at beginning of stitching and when you reach the mark (**Fig. 60**). Lift needle out of fabric and clip thread.

Fig. 60

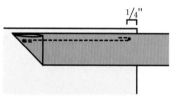

5. Fold binding as shown in **Figs. 61** and **62** and pin binding to adjacent side, matching raw edges. When you reach the next corner, mark ¹/₄" from edge of quilt.

Fig. 61   **Fig. 62**

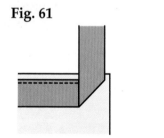

6. Backstitching at edge of quilt, sew pinned binding to quilt (**Fig. 63**); backstitch when you reach the next mark. Lift needle out of fabric and clip thread.

Fig. 63

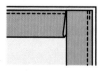

7. Repeat Steps 5 and 6 to continue sewing binding to quilt. Leaving a 2" overlap, trim excess binding. Stitch overlap in place.

8. On 1 edge of quilt, fold binding over to quilt backing and pin pressed edge in place, covering stitching line (**Fig. 64**). On adjacent side, fold binding over, forming a mitered corner (**Fig. 65**). Repeat to pin remainder of binding in place.

Fig. 64   **Fig. 65**

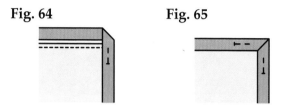

9. Blindstitch binding to backing.

ATTACHING BINDING WITH OVERLAPPED CORNERS

1. Matching raw edges and using a ¹/₄" seam allowance, sew 1 binding length to 1 edge on right side of quilt; trim ends of binding even with quilt. Fold binding over to quilt backing and pin pressed edge in place, covering stitching line (**Fig. 66**); blindstitch binding to backing. Repeat for opposite edge of quilt.

Fig. 66

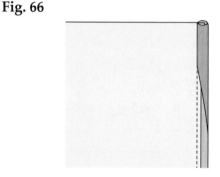

2. Leaving approximately 1¹/₂" at each end, stitch 1 binding length to 1 raw edge of quilt. Trim each end of binding ¹/₂" longer than bound edge. Fold each end of binding over to quilt backing (**Fig. 67**). Repeat for remaining edge.

Fig. 67

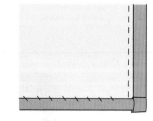

3. Fold binding over to quilt backing and blindstitch in place.

MAKING A HANGING SLEEVE

Attaching a hanging sleeve to the back of your wall hanging or quilt before the binding is added will allow you to use a dowel or wooden slat to display your completed project on a wall.

1. Measure the width of the wall hanging and subtract 1". Cut a piece of fabric 7"w by the determined measurement.
2. Press short edges of fabric piece 1/4" to wrong side; press edges 1/4" to wrong side again and machine stitch in place.
3. Matching wrong sides, fold piece in half lengthwise to form a tube.
4. Matching raw edges, baste hanging sleeve to center top edge on back of wall hanging.
5. Bind wall hanging as indicated in project instructions, treating the hanging sleeve as part of the backing.
6. Blindstitch bottom of hanging sleeve in place, taking care not to stitch through to front of quilt.
7. Insert dowel or slat into hanging sleeve.

SIGNING AND DATING YOUR QUILT

Your completed quilt is a work of art and should be treated as such. And like any other artist, you should sign and date your quilt. There are many different ways to do this, and you should pick a method of signing and dating that reflects the quilt, the occasion it was made for, and your own particular talents.

The following suggestions may give you an idea for recording the history of your quilt for future generations.

- Embroider your name, date, and any additional information on the quilt top or backing. You may use floss colors that closely match the fabric you are working on, such as white floss on a white border, or contrasting colors may be used.
- Make a label from muslin and use a permanent marker to write your information. Your label may be as plain or as fancy as you wish. Then stitch the label to the back of the quilt.
- Chart a cross-stitch label design that includes the information you wish and stitch it in colors that complement the quilt. Stitch the finished label to the quilt backing.

PILLOW FINISHING

Any quilt block may be made into a pillow. If desired, you may add a ruffle and/or welting to the pillow top before adding the backing.

MAKING THE PILLOW

1. For pillow back, cut a piece of fabric the same size as pieced and quilted pillow top.
2. Add welting or ruffle to pillow top as indicated in project instructions (see below).
3. Place pillow back and pillow top right sides together. Using a 1/2" seam allowance (or stitching as close as possible to welting), sew pillow top and back together, leaving an opening at bottom edge for turning. Turn pillow right side out, carefully pushing corners outward. Stuff with polyester fiberfill and sew final closure by hand.

ADDING WELTING

1. To make welting, measure outer dimensions of pillow top and add 2". Cut a bias strip of fabric 3"w by the determined measurement, piecing if necessary.
2. Lay cord along center of bias strip on wrong side of fabric; fold strip over cord. With zipper foot, machine baste along length of strip close to cord. Trim seam allowance to 1/2".
3. Matching raw edges and beginning and ending 3" from ends of welting, baste welting to right side of pillow top. To make turning corners easier, clip seam allowance of welting at pillow top corners.
4. Remove approximately 3" of seam at 1 end of welting; fold fabric away from cord. Trim remaining end of welting so that cord ends meet exactly. Fold short edge of welting fabric 1/2" to wrong side; fold fabric back over area where ends meet. Baste remainder of welting to pillow top close to cord.
5. Follow Step 3 of **Making the Pillow** to complete pillow.

ADDING A RUFFLE

1. To determine length of ruffle fabric, measure outer dimensions of pillow top and multiply by 2. To determine width of ruffle fabric, multiply the finished width measurement given in project instructions by 2 and add 1". Cut a strip of fabric the determined measurements, piecing if necessary.
2. Matching right sides, use a 1/4" seam allowance to sew short edges of ruffle together to form a large circle; press seam allowance open. To fold ruffle in half, match raw edges and fold 1 raw edge of fabric to inside of circle to meet remaining raw edge of fabric; press.

3. To gather ruffle, place quilting thread ¼" from raw edge of ruffle. Using a medium width zigzag stitch with medium stitch length, stitch over quilting thread, being careful not to catch quilting thread in stitching. Pull quilting thread, drawing up gathers to fit pillow top.

4. Matching raw edges, baste ruffle to right side of pillow top.

5. Follow Step 3 of **Making the Pillow**, page 157, to complete pillow.

EMBROIDERY STITCHES

Blanket Stitch
Come up at 1. Go down at 2 and come up at 3, keeping thread below point of needle (**Fig. 68**). Continue working as shown in **Fig. 69**.

Fig. 68   **Fig. 69**

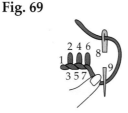

Feather Stitch
Come up at 1. Go down at 2 and come up at 3, keeping floss below point of needle (**Fig. 70**). Alternate stitches from right to left, keeping stitches symmetrical (**Fig. 71**).

Fig. 70   **Fig. 71**

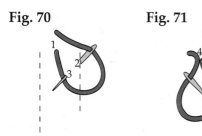

French Knot
Come up at 1. Wrap thread once around needle and insert needle at 2, holding end of thread with non-stitching fingers (**Fig. 72**). Tighten knot; then pull needle through, holding floss until it must be released. For larger knot, use more strands; wrap only once.

Fig. 72

Herringbone Stitch
Coming up at odd numbers and going down at even numbers, work evenly spaced stitches as shown in **Fig. 73**.

Fig. 73

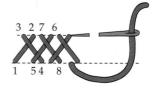

Stem Stitch
Come up at 1. Keeping thread below the stitching line, go down at 2 and come up at 3. Go down at 4 and up at 5 (same hole as 2) as shown in **Fig. 74**.

Fig. 74

Straight Stitch
Come up at 1 and go down at 2 (**Fig. 75**). Length of stitches may be varied as desired.

Fig. 75

Threaded Running Stitch
Work a line of running stitches. Using another length of same or contrasting thread, lace thread under running stitches as shown in **Fig. 76**, being careful not to catch fabric.

Fig. 76

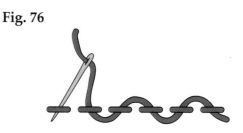

GLOSSARY

Appliqué — A cutout fabric shape that is sewn to a larger background.

Backing — The back or bottom layer of a quilt.

Backstitch — A reinforcing stitch taken at the beginning and end of a seam to secure stitches.

Basting — Large running stitches used to temporarily secure pieces or layers of fabric together. Basting is removed after permanent stitching.

Batting — The middle layer of a quilt; provides the insulation and warmth as well as the thickness.

Bias — The diagonal (45° for true bias) grain of fabric in relation to crosswise or lengthwise grain (see **Fig. 77**).

Binding — The fabric strip used to enclose the raw edges of the layered and quilted quilt. Also refers to the technique of finishing quilt edges in this way.

Border — Strips of fabric that are used to frame a quilt top.

Chain piecing — A machine-piecing method consisting of joining pairs of pieces one after the other by feeding them through the sewing machine without cutting the thread between the pairs.

Foundation piecing — A method of piecing that uses a fabric or paper foundation to which the pieces of the block are sewn.

Grain — The direction of the threads in woven fabric. "Crosswise grain" refers to the threads running from selvage to selvage. "Lengthwise grain" refers to the threads running parallel to the selvages (**Fig. 77**).

Fig. 77

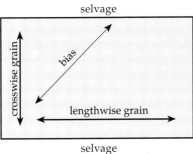

Machine baste — To baste using a sewing machine set at a long stitch length.

Miter — A method used to finish corners of quilt borders or bindings, consisting of joining fabric pieces at a 45° angle.

Piecing — Sewing together the pieces of a quilt design to form a quilt block or an entire quilt top.

Quilt block — Pieced or appliquéd sections that are sewn together to form a quilt top.

Quilt top — The decorative part of a quilt that is layered on top of the batting and backing.

Quilting — The stitching that holds together the 3 quilt layers (top, batting, and backing); or, the entire process of making a quilt.

Running stitch — A series of straight stitches with the stitch length equal to the space between stitches (**Fig. 78**).

Fig. 78

Sashing — Strips or blocks of fabric that separate individual blocks in a quilt top.

Seam allowance — The distance between the seam and the cut edge of the fabric. In quilting, this is usually ¼".

Selvages — The 2 finished lengthwise edges of fabric (see **Fig. 77**). Selvages should be trimmed from fabric before cutting.

Set (or Setting) — The arrangement of the quilt blocks as they are sewn together to form the quilt top.

Setting squares — Squares of plain (unpieced) fabric set between pieced or appliquéd quilt blocks in a quilt top.

Setting triangles — Triangles of fabric used around the outside of a diagonally-set quilt top to fill in between outer squares and border or binding.

Straight grain — The crosswise or lengthwise grain of fabric (see **Fig. 77**). The lengthwise grain has the least amount of stretch.

String quilt — A quilt pattern made up of many narrow strips ("strings") of fabric, often pieced using the foundation piecing method.

Template — A pattern used for marking quilt pieces to be cut out or for marking lines or designs for quilting.

Triangle-square — In piecing, 2 right triangles joined on their long sides to form a square with a diagonal seam (**Fig. 79**).

Fig. 79

Unit — A pieced section that is made as individual steps in the quilt construction process are completed. Units are usually combined to make blocks or other sections of the quilt top.

CREDITS

We want to extend a warm *thank you* to the generous people who allowed us to photograph our projects at their homes.

- *Churn Dash Collection*: Dr. Tony Johnson
- *Crown of Thorns*: Nancy Gunn Porter
- *String Collection*: Dan and Sandra Cook
- *Patriotic Collection*: Nancy Gunn Porter
- *Lone Star*: Dan and Sandra Cook
- *Amish Collection*: Nancy Gunn Porter
- *Spring Basket Collection*: Frank and Carol Clawson
- *Bold Collection*: Nancy Gunn Porter
- *Wild Goose Chase*: Thomas and Janet Feurig
- *Crib Quilts*: Mr. and Mrs. Shawn Fitz
- *Scottie Collection*: Susan Wildung
- *Log Cabin Collection*: John and Anne Childs
- *LeMoyne Star*: Susan Wildung
- *Ocean Waves*: Mary Anne Salmon

We also thank Ethan Allen Home Interiors, Little Rock, Arkansas, for allowing us to photograph our *Wild Rose Collection* in the store.

The LeMoyne Star Quilt, shown on page 116, is from the collection of Bryce and Donna Hamilton, Minneapolis, Minnesota.

We extend a special word of thanks to Constance Schlemeyer of Hallsville, Missouri, who created the Log Cabin Quilt shown on page 104.

We also want to thank Pam Bachus for the use of her Scottish terrier, which appears on pages 93 and 96.

To Magna IV Color Imaging of Little Rock, Arkansas, we say thank you for the superb color reproduction and excellent pre-press preparation.

We especially want to thank photographers Mark Mathews, Ken West, Larry Pennington, and Karen Busick Shirey of Peerless Photography, Little Rock, Arkansas, and Jerry R. Davis of Jerry Davis Photography, Little Rock, Arkansas, for their time, patience, and excellent work.

We extend a sincere *thank you* to all the people who assisted in making and testing the projects in this book: Karen Call, Debbie Chance, Nora Faye Clift, Stephanie Fite, Judith Hassed, Judith Kline, Barbara Middleton, Gazelle Mode, Sherri Mode, Ruby Solida, Karen Tyler, Dee Ann Younger, and the members of the First Assembly of God Church Women's Ministry, Searcy, Arkansas: Frances Blackburn, Louella English, Wanda Fite, Nan Goode, Bonnie Gowan, Juanita Hodges, Minnie Hogan, Ida Johnson, Ruby Johnson, Richadeen Lewis, Velrie Louks, Della Walters, and Minnie Whitehurst.